Managing for Investors in People

The Kogan Page Practical Trainer Series
Series Editor: Roger Buckley

'Excellent and challenging' The Learning World, BBC World Service
'Jargon-free and straightforward . . . sound advice' Personnel Management
'Clear, informative, very practically oriented' The Training Officer

Managing for Investors in People

PETER TAYLOR and BOB THACKWRAY

**KOGAN
PAGE**

London • Stirling (USA)

First published in 1997

Kogan Page Limited
120 Pentonville Road
London N1 9JN
and
22883 Quicksilver Drive
Stirling, VA 20166, USA

British Library Cataloguing in Publication Data

A CIP record for this book is available from the British Library.

ISBN 0 7494 2144 4

Typeset by Saxon Graphics Ltd, Derby
Printed and bound in Great Britain by Biddles Ltd, Guildford and King's Lynn

Contents

E0004966859001.

Acknowledgements

The authors gratefully acknowledge the contributions and support by a large number of individuals and organisations, especially:

Bill Flintham, Avesta Sheffield
Tom Reilly, Ealing, Hammersmith and Hounslow Health Authority
Lesley Wheeler, Excelsior Hotel, Heathrow
Norman Wragg, Health and Safety Laboratory, Sheffield
Doug Rogers, HPC Products, Stevenage
Tom Howe, IBM Education and Training
Dr David Wormald, Raflatac Limited, Scarborough
Paul Davies, Ramada Hotel, Heathrow

Introduction

What is Investors in People?

Investors in People is increasingly becoming recognised as the major standard for good practice in the development of people to achieve business success. By January 1997, just over five years after the first organisations achieved the Standard, some 5,200+ organisations have been recognised through the UK. In addition, some 22,000+ organisations are committed to become recognised and are actively working towards meeting its requirements. Together these organisations employ about 27% of the UK workforce.

It is not just happening in the UK, however. In early 1996 Investors in People was launched in Australia where, at the time of writing, six organisations have achieved recognition. Although not officially launched in any other countries, a great deal of interest is being shown in many European countries and in the US.

Why read this book?

This book is written with a number of purposes in mind.

1. To help organisations which are working towards Investors in People and need to gain the commitment of managers to carry out *their* responsibilities for managing the development of people.
2. To help managers at all levels:
   (a) understand how important their role is in helping organisations achieve Investors in People recognition;
   (b) be aware of the range of roles and responsibilities that they could be expected to have; and

(c) identify whether their own training and development to date has equipped them to carry out these roles and responsibilities.

3. For personnel and training specialists within organisations who are implementing Investors in People.

Who are the managers?

For the purpose of this book, 'manager' means anyone who is responsible for 'managing' the development of people. The term therefore includes everyone from first-line managers (ie, supervisors/team leaders, etc) to the most senior manager in the organisation (ie, the Managing Director/Chief Executive, etc). In most industrial sectors these terms will embrace most 'managers'. However, in some sectors different terminology might be used.

What does the book include?

The book further develops a theme outlined in the authors' previous book *Investors in People Explained* – the importance of the role of the manager in achieving Investors in People status. It is based on the practical experience the authors have gained working with a variety of organisations, all in the Investors in People process from implementation to assessment. Wherever possible it therefore includes illustrations from a variety of named organisations which have either achieved Investors in People status or are currently working towards it.

In Part I, Chapter 1 clarifies who managers are and examines the most common roles and responsibilities that managers have in managing the development of people and how these are changing. It looks at the range of skills and the knowledge and attributes effective managers need. Chapter 2 then considers what prevents managers from carrying out these roles and responsibilities and what benefits can be gained if they are carried out. It also examines what is meant by commitment (to developing people) from the top.

Chapter 3 examines the role of senior managers – who they are, whether they need additional skills and what their role is in achieving Investors in People status for their organisations.

Part II opens with Chapter 4, which examines communications. It considers why managers should communicate, what should be communicated and ends by detailing a variety of communications processes found by the authors in the course of their work as consultants and as Investors in People assessors.

Chapter 5 looks at identifying training and development needs and planning for evaluation. It details a number of approaches to identifying needs and also examines how managers' roles link to the roles and responsibilities of training and development specialists, where they exist. Next, Chapter 6 considers how 'development' fits in. It looks at what development is and details a number of different approaches and how to plan and structure development.

'Active support' from managers is discussed in Chapter 7. This chapter describes induction processes and examines coaching and feedback skills. Chapter 8 looks at evaluation, what it involves and some approaches that can be taken. The concluding chapter, Chapter 9, examines what managers need to do to help the organisation retain Investors in People recognition.

Finally, three appendices include the Investors in People Standard and an indicator-by-indicator explanation of what an assessor would expect to see managers doing, sources of help available for organisations and a sample evaluation form.

How to use this book

Most chapters are self-contained to enable readers to dip in and out of the book if they wish to do so. However, it is a good idea to read Chapter 1 first as understanding who the manager is will be important for the rest of the book. Following the summary at the end of most chapters is a list of the actions required by managers and the Investors in People indicators that are relevant to the content of the chapter.

Before starting, readers might like to consider the questions in the survey on page 4. It might also be interesting to ask employees the same questions and compare responses.

Poldark Graham INVESTORS IN PEOPLE: MANAGERS' SURVEY

Please tick the most relevant of the boxes on the right.

		Yes	No	Unsure
1.	Is the company committed to training and developing its people?	☐	☐	☐
2.	Do you have a clear vision of how the company will develop?	☐	☐	☐
3.	If yes, has it been communicated to all your employees?	☐	☐	☐
4.	Does your company have a written business plan?	☐	☐	☐
5.	Does your company have a written plan which identifies broad training and development needs?	☐	☐	☐
6.	Is everyone in your team clear how their role contributes to helping the company meet its business plan?	☐	☐	☐
7.	Has the company trained and developed you to manage the development of your staff?	☐	☐	☐
8.	Are the training needs of *all* your employees reviewed on a regular basis?	☐	☐	☐
9.	Does this review lead to:			
	(a) a training plan for your team;	☐	☐	☐
	(b) a personal training and development plan for all your employees?	☐	☐	☐
10.	Do you actively encourage and support all your employees in developing their skills?	☐	☐	☐
11.	Is there an induction programme for all new employees?	☐	☐	☐
12.	Do you 'induct' people who are transferred from other parts of the company?	☐	☐	☐
13.	Before training and/or development activities do you agree what you expect in terms of new skills or knowledge?	☐	☐	☐
14.	Following training and/or development activities do you			
	(a) review that the activity met its objectives;	☐	☐	☐
	(b) ensure that employees are using any newly acquired skills or knowledge?	☐	☐	☐
15.	Do you assess the costs and benefits of training and development activities?	☐	☐	☐
16.	Do you believe that you are effective in managing the development of your employees?	☐	☐	☐

Part 1 The Managers

1 Who are the Managers?

This chapter is essential reading as it sets the scene for the whole book. It examines where the responsibility for managing people to achieve Investors in People status actually lies. It moves on to consider what these responsibilities comprise in most organisations and how they are subject to change. It also examines how they link to the role of training specialists, where they exist.

The additional responsibilities that senior managers have with regard to managing the development of people are dealt with in Chapter 3.

What is a manager and who is included?

Among a number of definitions the *Oxford English Dictionary* defines a manager as: 'a person who is in charge of the affairs of a business etc'. For the purposes of Investors in People, and therefore for this book, the term 'manager' includes anyone who has responsibility for managing the development of people. It includes everyone from first-line managers to the most senior person within the organisation.

Generally, the term 'manager' can include team leader, supervisor, chargehand, foreman, etc. In some sectors, education for example, there are specific roles identified such as headteacher, Deans of Faculty, Heads of Schools. Within health, Ward Managers, Sisters, Staff Nurses, General Practitioners and Practice Managers would be included. In organisations such as solicitors' or accountants' practices it includes the partners, although many set up alternative arrangements to manage the development of support staff.

What are the most common responsibilities of managers?

The broad responsibilities of managers have been established for a long time and, until recently, have changed very little over the years. We can now categorise these responsibilities or functions under four headings:

- managing tasks
- managing resources
- managing people
- managing information.

As this book is concerned with managing for Investors in People, we are concentrating on those responsibilities concerned with managing people; in particular the development of people.

At the end of most chapters and in Appendix 1 we examine what managers actually need to do in order to help organisations achieve Investors in People status.

The responsibilities

The following list of key responsibilities associated with the management of people is drawn from contributions made by participants on a number of management development programmes. They are not presented in any order of priority.

- Communicating
- Identifying and agreeing training needs
- Planning to meet those needs
- Implementing action to meet the needs
- Coaching/mentoring
- Monitoring
- Resourcing
- Empowering and involving.

The following skills, knowledge and attributes required to manage the development of people were also identified.

The skills

- communication skills (eg, questioning, listening, clarifying, presenting, influencing, feedback, counselling)
- leadership
- team building – rapport building

- planning/organising/forecasting
- time management
- motivating
- problem solving – analytical, assessing
- decision-making skills
- coaching/training
- controlling
- delegating.

Knowledge requirements

- the organisation
- the jobs
- the people
- the 'rules'
- the policies
- the resources.

Attributes

- firmness
- honesty
- enthusiasm
- fairness
- credibility
- consistency
- tact/diplomacy
- being a 'people person'.

This highlights the vast range of skills and knowledge necessary to be an effective manager of people and, therefore, their development. The reader may be forgiven, after reading this, for thinking that superhuman powers are required. Clearly a manager does not need to be an expert in all these areas, but to be effective, managers need to have a reasonable working knowledge of these skills in their toolkit so that they can be called upon when the need arises.

Surveys of participants on management development programmes asking for information on what training and development they had received to enable them to carry out these responsibilities revealed a mixed picture, ranging from none to a considerable amount. Significantly, however, the majority of people were at the lower end of the continuum.

Of course there are many more items that could be added to the list of skills and knowledge but we have restricted ourselves to adding just two more: *the management of change* and *project management*. These are of considerable significance as all organisations are living with continual change, both internally and externally. Increased competition, spiralling costs, major policy changes, cuts in funding and a range of other factors conspire to create a fast moving and fast changing environment and managers are at the forefront of these changes and may well bear the brunt of the accompanying pressures. They need to help their people to cope with change and quite often this involves managing project teams.

The changing role of managers

Organisations are not the only things that are changing: managers themselves are facing huge changes. Michael Hammer, in *Re-engineering the Corporation,* summarises one essential change as being the move from being supervisors to being coaches. This is in line with the recurrent theme in much of the current thinking on the role of people at work, ie, from *'controlled* to *empowered'*.

Two key strategies employed by organisations that impact significantly on the role of managers are delayering and decentralisation.

Delayering/flattening structures

By far the most common strategy involves organisations questioning the need for large numbers of managers at different levels. There are many reasons for this happening but two factors stand out as major contributors to the development of the situation.

First, the increased use of technology has made the gathering and utilisation of management information a far more refined process. Indeed, the sophistication of the activity is such that in many organisations the Tom Peters' view, put forward in *In Search of Excellence,* that evaluation is the conversion of hindsight into management information, is firmly built into everyday working practices.

Second, there is a clearly measurable trend to push more and more responsibility 'down the line'. Regardless of the initial impetus (eg, whether or not it is Total Quality Management driven or cost led) it is on the increase. As people accept this responsibility, several of the functions that formerly comprised part of the manager's role became self-managed by the work force. Therefore, fewer managers are required.

In some organisations whole strata of managers have disappeared as staff have become more 'empowered' and have taken responsibilities and, therefore, functions away from the management role.

Decentralising the personnel and training and development functions

As these layers of management disappear, a number of organisations have started to question the need for in-house training and development specialists. Many specialist functions can be devolved to (properly trained and developed) managers. If responsibility is to be transferred as far down the organisation as possible, inevitably organisations are asking why not do the same with the personnel and training and development functions? In theory, as mentioned earlier, managers have always had training and development responsibilities. Research has shown that training and development, such as it was, was delivered with varying degrees of success. Experience has shown that the existence of specialists within the organisation led to a number of managers abdicating that particular responsibility in practice. Indeed, a similar phenomenon can be observed in some organisations with regard to their Investors in People 'champion'.

Value statements

Finally, another recent trend influencing the role of the manager is the increased and increasing emphasis on the introduction of 'value statements' by organisations. For many years the leading-edge companies have used value statements. For example, since the 1950s Toyota has had an operating philosophy based on a number of values such as:

- the customer always comes first
- quality applies to everything Toyota does
- respect for the value of people.

Inevitably when these value statements are introduced they need commitment from managers at all levels to implement them effectively. They also have an impact on management behaviour. This is, of course, especially true when the value statement relates to how people are treated and valued.

The new skill requirements for managers

Managers in the type of organisation described above have a quite different role to the traditional one. To succeed, and be secure, the modern manager has to be seen to be 'adding value'. They need to help to integrate quality, to be innovative and, as mentioned above, to manage change. This new role also involves facilitating and supporting their people rather than policing and controlling them. The contemporary manager will be responsible for encouraging and empowering their people to manage themselves within a broad framework. Employees are encouraged to seek improvements through innovation and challenging the status quo. Many managers find this uncomfortable. It may seem ironic, but as employees are empowered many managers need considerable support and encouragement from their own manager in order to develop and practice these new skills and attitudes.

The role of training specialists

Where organisations do retain training and development specialists, it is necessary to avoid managers being tempted to abdicate their responsibility for training and development. Therefore, it is important to clearly state what the responsibilities of managers actually are and how they then link to those of the training specialist. Most organisations would simply say that managers are responsible for ensuring that their people have the skills and knowledge to carry out their role. The training specialist is responsible for *supporting* managers in fulfilling their responsibilities.

Where training specialists do not exist in organisations, managers will need to ensure that training does take place. However, they do not have to deliver the training. The training is often carried out by people to whom they have delegated appropriate responsibility.

Of course, nominated employees should themselves be trained to carry out these additional responsibilities, although our experience suggests that this is often not the case.

In Chapter 3 we discuss the additional responsibilities that senior managers have for the development of people.

Summary

This chapter has reviewed the current and changing roles and responsibilities of managers relating to the development of people. It has considered what skills, knowledge and attributes managers require to fulfil these responsibilities.

References

Hammer, M and Champy, J (1993) *Reengineering the Corporation – A manifesto for business revolution*, London: Nicholas Brearley.

Peters, T and Waterman, R (1982) *In Search of Excellence*, Harper & Row, New York.

THE RELEVANT INVESTORS IN PEOPLE INDICATORS

1.1 The commitment from top management to train and develop employees is communicated effectively throughout the organisation.

2.5 Responsibility for training and developing employees is clearly identified and understood throughout the organisation, starting at the top.

3.2 Managers are effective in carrying out their responsibilities for training and developing employees.

3.3 Managers are actively involved in supporting employees to meet their training and development needs.

2 The Manager and Training and Development

This chapter is essential reading. It examines the barriers preventing managers from carrying out the roles and responsibilities identified in Chapter 1. It considers how commitment – or lack of it – from senior managers can affect their role. It also examines the benefits managers can gain if they do train and develop their people.

What are the barriers?

The most obvious and commonly quoted reason for not managing the development of people is lack of time and/or pressure of work. Clearly the pressures on the contemporary manager are much greater today than they were some years ago, especially as there are often less of them! Did managers actually spend any more time developing people 20 years ago than they do now?

That is not to say that training did not take place. The training and development of people has historically been moving towards centre stage since the rise of the Mechanics Institutes during the first part of the last century. At one time, in fact, training and development was done in secret – if you were found out you would face the sack and if you organised the training there were possible legal penalties!

Other reasons often quoted for not developing staff are:

- 'Top management merely pay lip service to training and development.'
- 'It's not my job – it's the training department's job.'
- 'If I train my staff too well I'll lose them.'
- 'Developed staff are more challenging/threatening.'
- Lack of resources, especially money.

- Lack of support or encouragement from their line manager.
- Lack of confidence or understanding.
- Overcomplicated or unnecessary systems.
- 'It's not the way things are done round here.'
- Failure to see/understand the benefits.
- Lack of training and development.

Lack of commitment from the top to training and development

The first indicator in the Investors in People Standard is:

'The commitment from top management to train and develop employees is communicated effectively throughout the organisation.'

Without this evident commitment from the top it makes it more difficult for managers to carry out their responsibilities. If managers themselves are publicly questioning this commitment then that organisation will not satisfy an assessor and will not, therefore, be recognised as an Investor in People.

We, as assessors and advisers ourselves, have experienced this situation in many organisations. This occurs mainly in those organisations which are working towards recognition but occasionally in those which have applied to be assessed.

It is evident that a number of senior managers feel that all they have to do to demonstrate commitment to training and development is to make a statement such as 'people are our greatest asset'. They then do very little else to convince their people to believe that this is true.

In those organisations where senior managers have always been committed to training and development, this statement may be unnecessary or may have already been made in a variety of locally meaningful ways. For those organisations where it has not been evident that this commitment exists, there is a need to change culture/custom/practice to demonstrate to all staff that investing in people is real and is valued as good practice by the organisation.

All managers have a significant role to play here but it is ridiculous to expect managers to reinforce this commitment with their people if they are not convinced themselves. Clearly, therefore, the process needs to begin by convincing the managers themselves and creating the 'climate' for training and development to take place.

There is no one simple answer: the message must be constantly reinforced by action. Senior managers in organisations which have been recognised do a variety of things that demonstrate this commitment, a theme also picked up in Chapter 3.

Being visible is a good starting point but in very large organisations this is not easy. A number of recognised large organisations have produced videos to get the message across but nothing beats being seen in person. For many years Tom Peters has promoted 'managing by walking about'; this is an extension of the same idea. Again it is not easy in large organisations but they generally have a large top team so it can be shared out between them.

Being visible is only part of the process. If nothing happens as a result then people will still not be convinced, so the next stage in demonstrating commitment is to ensure that meeting training and development needs is adequately resourced.

It is quite common to hear comments such as 'top management are committed until they have to put their hands in their pockets.' Managers and their people will finally be convinced when identified training and development actually takes place.

Opportunities to access training and development need to be distributed equitably. As assessors and advisers, we often hear comments such as:

'it's OK if you work on the shop floor'
'they're only committed to training technicians'
'if you're in admin you're a second-class citizen'.

Clearly if the amount of training and development needed is huge it will have to be prioritised. Those whose needs do not fall into the top priority must understand this to avoid comments such as, 'yes we have a process for identifying training needs but nothing ever happens'.

The following illustrations show how commitment from managers was demonstrated to employees in two organisations, both recognised as Investors in People.

When IBM Education Business and Training (formerly IBM Education Services Business) made the commitment to work towards Investors in People they considered how best to demonstrate their commitment to their employees. It was decided that the managers should make a declaration to their employees. This declaration, shown in Figure 2.1, was signed by all the managers and reproductions were framed and displayed around the buildings.

The second illustration concerns the Excelsior Hotel at Heathrow. Going for Investors in People coincided with the introduction of a customer care programme. A mission statement and a statement of

---

TOWARDS INVESTMENT IN PEOPLE: MANAGERS' DECLARATION

'The effective development and training of all employees in the Education Services Business is of paramount importance.

Therefore we will ensure that everyone has a training plan relevant to the needs of the business and of the individual.

In doing this we will follow the National Standard for "Investors in People";

we will continue to encourage external accreditation;

and we will support the ESB Vision for Employee Development described below and the plan presented on 28th April 1994.'

In the journey towards the ESB vision we will achieve the following for Employee Development:

1. *'Investors in People' Award.*
2. *External accreditation.*
3. *Baldrige (Bronze) Award.*
4. *Development plans in place.*
5. *Creation of individual CVs.*
6. *External recognition.*

SIGNATURES:

24/5/94

Figure 2.1 *Managers' declaration of commitment*

values had been drawn up but it was felt action needed to be taken in order to gain the commitment of staff and convince them that managers were committed to the values.

The concept of a 'Passport to Excellence' was developed. A passport-size document was produced containing:

- a copy of the Excelsior mission and values
- a place to put a 'smiling' photograph
- Ten Management Commitments, signed by the departmental manager
- a space for the team member to enter and sign for 'team member commitments'
- space for the passport to be 'stamped' as the team member attended customer care training modules
- space for other training to be entered and stamped.

The Ten Management Commitments are as follows:

- I will seek your opinions and suggestions and implement feasible ideas.
- I will have an open door policy ready to listen – help – support.
- I will ensure that you are free to attend nominated training courses.
- I will allow you to make decisions within guidelines.
- I will be both a team coach and team player.
- I will give you the training and equipment that will enable you to do your job with confidence.
- I will review your development every six months and give you feedback.
- I will share my objectives and those of the team with you.
- I will inform you of business plans and performance for the Company, the Hotel and Department.
- I will smile.

What's in it for managers?

In many organisations, including a number that we have worked with, it is clear that there is a commitment from the top, yet some managers still do not manage the development of their people effectively.

The managers who ask the question, 'What's in it for me?' are usually those managers who are totally focused on getting the job done. They are often referred to as 'task' managers. Task managers exist in all organisations and at all levels, including the senior team.

Clearly every manager is there to ensure the task is completed: if the job is not done the organisation may cease to exist. However, task managers concentrate on getting the job done to such an extent that they often ignore the needs of their people. They are likely to be experts in the task but not at 'managing'. They may well have learnt to manage by observing other task managers and, either by choice or lack of opportunity, have had little training in management techniques. They are not good listeners, they probably believe no one can do the job as well as they can, and if there are problems they will say things such as 'Leave it to me, I'll sort it out' or 'Why do I have to do everything myself?' They tend not to trust their staff so delegate very little and invariably they work extremely hard – because they do almost everything themselves, sometimes even routine tasks.

Convincing these managers that training and developing their people has benefits is very difficult. Probably having had little training themselves, they wonder why other people should need it. The benefits of investing in their people to these managers are potentially huge.

If they *invest* time with their people in training and developing, through sharing their expertise with them, they will find problems don't occur as often because people have been shown how to anticipate them. When they do occur, unless it is a new or critical problem they will be able to deal with it themselves because they will have learnt how to handle it. This releases the pressure and allows the manager to devote more time to dealing with the really critical issues.

The chief danger associated with a task manager is that people become demotivated and mistakes are more likely to occur. People know that their manager will always 'sort things out' if things go wrong. Others may feel that there is little point in showing initiative because things usually go wrong when they do. This may well be the case because they don't fully understand the impact of their actions as it has never been discussed with them.

So, for the task manager the biggest benefit from training and developing staff is likely to be more time – and therefore resource availability – in the longer term.

There is a lot of satisfaction to be gained from developing people. It is possible that developed people will move on to better jobs but in the shorter term the manager who develops people will have benefited in a variety of ways from, for example, having taken someone with few skills and little knowledge and helped their development by passing on their own expertise.

People who have been developed – and are aware that they have been developed – usually appreciate it. They are usually very committed to doing a good job and often stay longer in the job because they get a great deal of satisfaction. If they do decide they need to move on to a more 'stretching' job the manager can derive satisfaction from knowing they have played a key role in helping the person develop and can look forward to starting again with a new person. '*People*' managers naturally feel this satisfaction; although they probably feel some regrets about losing a good member of staff they will still take pride in having done a good job as a people manager. '*Task*' managers will probably feel that if they hadn't developed them so well the person may not have left. However, this statement clearly suggests that if you don't train staff they'll stay! Research shows that, especially with new starters, the most commonly cited reason for leaving is *lack of adequate* training. This does not always mean they have not had any training but that the training was not felt to be good enough.

Indeed, some organisations place a very high premium on training and development, especially at the initial induction stage. One example is Hewlett Packard, which has an intensive induction over several weeks and underpins its commitment to developing its people with the view that it is better to have excellence for a short time than mediocrity for a lifetime.

Managers who have high staff turnover (or absenteeism) in their teams will find the investment in training and development will pay off quite quickly. Huge savings in time spent on the initial training can be made if they have a more stable team.

Overcoming the 'lack of time' barrier

If you believe in the benefits you will overcome the barriers and make time! This is easy to say but it is true.

Managers who are convinced that the investment in time will pay off find the time even if it means a lot of extra effort in the short term. They will also find the resources. If they are not getting the support from their own manager they will make the case in order to get that support. If the case is well made it would be a very unreasonable manager who failed to support it, especially if they are committed to the value of training and development themselves!

Frequently a lack of time problem is made worse by systems being too complicated or unnecessary. In organisations that are committed to training and developing their people we have found that the 'culture' encourages the need for complicated systems to be challenged. If they are essential it will be explained why and, even though it may not help time problems, at least people understand the rationale. But if they are not essential then they quite often are changed or scrapped altogether. The myth of bureaucracy being associated with Investors in People is just not true.

Training and development for managers

We have already looked at the skills and knowledge required by managers to manage effectively the development of their people.

Quite often management training courses are filled by people who have these skills and knowledge and are quite capable of managing their people but are looking for additional skills and ideas. Experience has shown that the managers who lack some of these skills and knowledge and really need management training and development rarely volunteer for it. The onus therefore is really on senior managers to identify the training and development needs of their managers and ensure that they are met. This does not always mean they should attend a lot of training courses, but merely require coaching and development on the job.

Managers do not have to be expert trainers and developers but must have a broad understanding of some of the basic principles. They should understand the principles of coaching. An outline has been included in Chapter 7.

Summary

This chapter has looked at reasons why managers do not always effectively manage the development of their people. It has looked at the need for top level commitment to training and development and what it entails. It has examined the benefits to managers of training and developing their people. Finally it made some suggestions that may overcome the remaining barriers that prevent managers carrying out their responsibilities.

Reference

Peters, T and Waterman, R (1982) *In Search of Excellence*, Harper & Row, New York.

THE RELEVANT INVESTORS IN PEOPLE INDICATORS

1.1 The commitment from top management to train and develop employees is communicated effectively throughout the organisation.

1.3 The organisation has considered what employees at all levels will contribute to the success of the organisation, and has communicated this effectively to them.

2.2 A written plan identifies the organisation's training and development needs, and specifies what action will be taken to meet these needs.

2.3 Training and development needs are regularly reviewed against goals and targets at the organisation, team and individual level.

2.4 A written plan identifies the resources that will be used to meet training and development needs.

3.2 Managers are effective in carrying out their responsibilities for training and developing employees.

3.3 Managers are actively involved in supporting employees to meet their training and development needs.

3.4 All employees are made aware of the training and development opportunities open to them.

3.5 All employees are encouraged to help identify and meet their job-related training and development needs.

---

3 The Role of Senior Managers

This chapter looks at the responsibilities for training and development of senior managers in organisations which are working towards Investors in People.

Who are senior managers?

Most organisations have a team of managers who are considered to be the Senior Management Team. Where the line is drawn between managers and senior managers will vary from one organisation to another. For the purposes of this book they are the team that set strategies and policies and manage (or direct) the managers of the organisation.

The responsibilities of senior managers

Some work is currently being carried out on behalf of the Management Charter Initiative (MCI) to develop standards for senior managers. The key purpose of senior managers has been described by MCI as: 'to develop and implement strategies to further the organisation's mission'. It goes on to describe the key issues for senior managers as:

- understanding and influencing the environment
- setting the strategy and gaining commitment
- planning, implementing and monitoring
- evaluating and improving performance.

They also have a responsibility to manage the development of the people who report directly to them but they also set the strategies and policies for *all* people in the organisation.

The skills, knowledge and attributes required of senior managers

Chapter 1 of this book describes what managers identified as the skills, knowledge and attributes that they need to manage the development of their people. A close examination should reveal that, *to manage the development of their people*, senior managers require in the main the same skills and attributes although, as they set the rules, policies, etc for organisations, the knowledge requirements may be different.

They clearly need to have strategic skills which in terms of developing people will embrace such things as succession planning, management development and other global people issues.

They need to agree policies on induction, qualifications and management responsibilities for the development of people. While these may have been the responsibility of the Personnel Manager in some organisations, the responsibility for personnel matters is being devolved and personnel specialists are themselves either disappearing or taking on additional responsibilities. This leads to senior managers requiring a range of new skills and knowledge.

We feel, based on feedback gained through interviewing employees at all levels in organisations, that a large proportion of senior managers are not as effective in managing the development of people as they should be. They tend to assume that middle managers are quite capable of managing their own development and while this should be true to some extent, middle managers in many organisations are being asked to do a great deal more than they have ever done before and need lots of support from their managers. However, middle managers in many organisations are an endangered species and are therefore unlikely to seek too much support as it may be seen as a sign of weakness.

Commitment to training and development from the top

There is a tendency for senior managers to be 'task managers' rather than 'people managers' and therefore to overlook the development needs of their people. This also leads to a possible conclusion that they are unlikely to be as committed to developing people as they should be. Alternatively, they consider themselves committed but their actions undermine their commitment because everything they do and say reinforces their commitment to the task, rather than the people.

Chapter 2 examined how the absence of commitment to training and development from the senior managers can form a barrier, or a ready-made excuse, to the commitment of middle managers. As well as undermining their commitment it may also affect the development of middle managers.

Even when senior managers *are* committed to training and development it can be undermined by previous 'initiatives' that they have been committed to. This often results in comments such as, 'I've heard it all before' or, 'I am sure they are committed, but nothing ever happens' from managers and their people. Initiative overload seems to be quite common in many organisations at the moment. The outcome is that many initiatives are not seen through to the end and people become very cynical about the next 'initiative' or 'flavour of the month'.

Evaluation at senior manager/organisational level

The Investors in People Standard specifically requires senior managers to be aware of the costs and benefits of training and developing their people. This means that they should to some extent be involved in, or at least aware of, the evaluation of training at the organisational level. This means that from time to time training and development should feature on the agenda of meetings of the Senior Management Team.

As part of the planning process they should identify the broad training and development needed to achieve the business plan. This should at least include strategies to cover health and safety and other relevant legislation; management development strategies; the introduction or expansion of IT and the related training. In many organisations it will include looking at aspects associated with quality and customer care that inevitably affect everybody in an organisation.

They should ensure that they are aware in broad terms of the impact that training and development are having on the organisation's performance, the benefits gained and whether they have received value for money for the resources allocated. This inevitably means having some process for collating information gathered through management channels.

Summary

This chapter has reviewed the responsibilities of senior managers in organisations who are working towards Investors in People status. It has examined the requirements in terms of additional skills and knowledge and outlined what they should actually do to reinforce their commitment to the process.

What do senior managers need to do?

To reinforce their commitment, whenever possible senior managers should:

- be visible and show that they are committed to training and development in both formal and informal discussions with staff
- ensure that there are adequate resources in terms of time, people and money to meet those training and development needs that have been identified
- take every opportunity to recognise and reinforce the valuable contribution people make to business success
- ensure all people understand that there are developmental opportunities available that contribute to the development of skills or knowledge needed to meet business requirements
- ensure that 'initiatives' are seen through to the end
- tackle those middle managers who are *not* committed.

They need to:

- plan and agree policies at an organisational level that consider the broad training and developmental needs required to achieve the business objectives
- as part of monitoring business performance, review progress of the broad impact of the planned training and developmental activity, including the roles and responsibilities of managers
- continually reinforce the contribution training and development make to business success
- celebrate the success of training and development
- periodically restate their commitment to continue to train and develop people because it pays to do so.

THE RELEVANT INVESTORS IN PEOPLE INDICATORS

All indicators (see Appendix 1) are relevant to senior managers, but particular attention should be paid to:

1.1 The commitment from top management to train and develop employees is communicated effectively throughout the organisation.

1.2 Employees at all levels are aware of the broad aims or vision of the organisation.

1.3 The employer has considered what employees at all levels will contribute to the success of the organisation, and has communicated this effectively to them.

2.1 A written but flexible plan sets out the organisation's goals and targets.

2.2 A written plan identifies the organisation's training and development needs, and specifies what action will be taken to meet these needs.

2.3 Training and development needs are regularly reviewed against goals and targets at the *organisation*, team and individual level.

2.4 A written plan identifies the resources that will be used to meet training and development needs.

2.5 Responsibility for training and developing employees is clearly identified and understood throughout the organisation, starting at the top.

4.3 The organisation evaluates the contribution of training and development to the achievement of its goals and targets.

4.4 Top management understands the broad costs and benefits of training and developing employees.

4.6 Top management's continuing commitment to training and developing employees is demonstrated to all employees.

Part 2 Managing the Process

4 Communication

This chapter develops a number of issues raised in previous chapters. It:

- considers what the manager needs to do to manage the process of training and developing their people. It starts by examining *the* key management tool – communication
- outlines some methods of communication used by organisations, the manager's role as a communicator and how this links to commitment to training and development.

Why communicate?

We have found that no matter how good (or bad) communications are in organisations, people will invariably say they could be better. In that case, why bother?

Research has shown that the most effective organisations are the ones that communicate with their employees on a regular basis. The theory, borne out by research, is that if people understand what the organisation is trying to do and how they can contribute to its success they will generally be more committed and therefore be more motivated to want to help the organisation succeed. In a recent seminar, Ricardo Semler, author of the best selling book *Maverick*, said 'the single hardest thing to do is to make people interested in coming to work on Monday morning'. We believe that effective and open communication contributes greatly to overcoming this difficulty.

There are, of course, people who have no wish to be well informed. It would be naive to believe that it is possible to gain the whole-hearted commitment of everyone who works for the organisation. A large number of people are quite happy to go to work, do their job and go home. They believe they can tell how well the company is doing by the orders that are going out of the door. They are not really interested in what's happening in any part of the company but their own. They have never been communicated with in the past so why should they bother listening now? They may well be suspicious of the motives of management who suddenly decide to adopt a more 'open' approach to communication.

There are not many employees who genuinely fall into this category, and their numbers are diminishing. The typical stereotype of this category is the long-serving worker in a traditional industry. When organisations decide to commit to Investors in People, however, it is these people who may cause their managers a significant amount of local difficulty.

What are the key messages to communicate?

We have found that significant numbers of people do appreciate the fact that communications are improving and senior managers are disclosing more about how well the organisation is doing and what the future plans are. Of course there will be cases where future plans may not be entirely in keeping with what employees want, but clearly they are better being informed than kept in the dark or misinformed by rumour and speculation.

Like the Excelsior Hotel mentioned in Chapter 2, most organisations have vision statements, mission statements and, increasingly, value statements. Ideally these should have been developed in consultation with the workforce, as was the case in the Excelsior. In practice they are often developed by senior managers or in some organisations through events involving all managers. In such situations, it is essential that the meaning and purpose of such statements are communicated effectively to all employees. If they are not communicated, why have them?

We have discovered that a number of organisations communicate their statements through impressive launches and do little else. To get employees to understand and to 'own' the messages in the statements it is important that they are continually reinforced. This means that every message should either directly or indirectly include aspects of the vision, mission or values. As any marketing specialist will tell you, 'it is not the weight of the water that wears away the stone, it is the drip, drip drip...'

Effective communication should ensure that all people understand how they contribute to the success of the organisation, and reinforce senior managers' commitment to training and developing people and how this has contributed – and will continue to contribute – to business success.

Setting the context for training and development

Another important reason for communicating the future plans of the organisation is that it sets the context for training and development actions. One of the main benefits expressed by organisations who have been recognised as Investors in People is the added focus it has given them in terms of setting business objectives and relating training and development to them. It has ensured that training and development activity is understood to be relevant to the needs of the organisation. In some organisations it can reduce expenditure on training and development when it is discovered that some elements of the activity were not in line with the organisation's objectives.

To enable individuals and their managers to relate training and development to the organisation's needs, these needs have to be communicated in the first place. Figure 4.1 illustrates how this works in a large number of organisations.

The model has been simplified to show the communication process once organisations have clarified their broad aims and vision. This has, in turn, enabled them to devise objectives, usually as part of a plan. This is then communicated to enable the people and their managers to agree relevant training and development actions. Then a training and development plan can be drawn up at the organisational level.

Communication processes also present the chance to ensure people are aware of other developmental opportunities open to them, such as seeking external qualifications or engaging in other developmental activities such as conferences, exhibitions, etc.

What methods of communication are there?

In very small, single-site organisations, communications should not be a problem, at least in theory, as people constantly work close together.

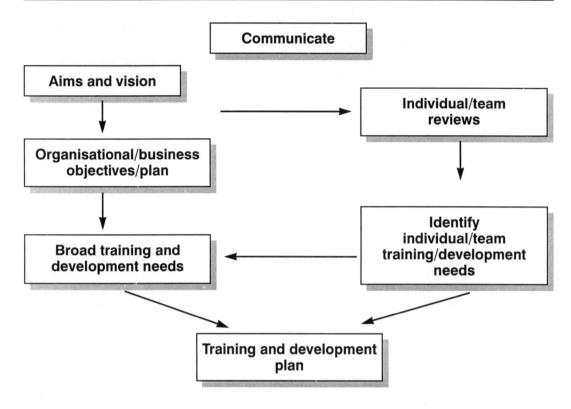

Figure 4.1 *A model for identifying and communicating business and training and development needs*

The senior manager/management is probably very visible and the opportunity to communicate is constantly available. Clearly this is not the case in larger organisations or those that are geographically dispersed. These organisations need to either be more structured in their communications processes or, in some cases, more imaginative.

Team briefings

An increasing number of organisations, especially large ones, are using a formal team briefing process as the method of passing messages to the workforce.

The process will normally involve passing on information, usually on a monthly basis. The information will outline current achievements against the plan and what the next month's targets may be. In addition, senior managers will normally agree what key messages need to be passed on to the workforce; these form the 'core brief'. These may include an outline of future plans and strategies, adjustments to plans, market influences, etc. Team briefs often include information about the people, eg, leavers, retirements and new starters.

The message in the core brief can be passed on unaltered to all employees but managers may wish to add a 'local flavour' as the message is cascaded down throughout the organisation. This cascade process normally starts with a member of the senior team briefing the presenters, who will have been trained for this role. In many organisations these 'team briefers' are managers, but this does not always have to be the case. To ensure that everyone gets the message a transcript of the brief is normally made available so that absentees can read it.

With the growth of new technology, such as networked computer systems, e-mail and intranets, many organisations are able to circulate copies of the briefs electronically. This offers the potential to make the process more interactive and to avoid the accusation that 'there is no communication, just information'.

Team briefing systems normally include, and encourage, employees to use the system to ask questions and pass messages and concerns back up to senior management.

Advantages of team briefings include:

- consistent messages are passed on to all the workforce
- the formality of the system ensures that the process works and happens on a regular basis
- there are possibilities for integration into team meetings where they exist.

Disadvantages include:

- as team briefings go down through an organisation they get longer and longer as the local flavour is added – managers may find it difficult or be frightened to précis the brief
- not presenting information about the organisation's performance in simple terms; this is invariably off-putting to most of the recipients
- the system does not lend itself to certain types of organisations eg, continuous process operations, shift working or geographically dispersed organisations, where the challenges of getting everyone together at the same time are almost insurmountable

- excessive reliance on the quality of the presentation of the 'briefer'. In practice, a large number of organisations do not get as many messages passed back up through the system as they would like.

However, we have found really effective team briefing processes. These occur when briefers have been well trained and are able to facilitate discussion that enables employees to interpret how 'core' messages are likely to impact on their roles.

Regular team meetings, notice boards, etc

Given that the idea of team meetings is hardly a new one, it is surprising how many organisations have not used them or have allowed them to fall into disuse.

Team meetings may not be as formal as team briefings. This can be both an advantage and a disadvantage. The informality can enable a meeting to be called at short notice while an issue is current, but lack of structure can also allow such gatherings to run out of steam.

The most effective team meetings are those that are held on a regular basis, perhaps on a fixed date each month, with short but relevant agendas, some of which may have been set by the team itself.

Although many organisations have used notice boards for years, we have found that their use in some organisations has been viewed as quite radical. They should not be seen as *the* method of communicating but as a supplement to other methods. It is, of course, difficult to check whether messages are getting through if they are the sole means of communicating with the workforce.

Newsletters, in-house journals, memos, etc

These present ideal vehicles for getting messages across in organisations that are geographically dispersed, where the workforce are outstationed or working from home. Again, there is nothing new about these processes but it is amazing how many organisations do not use them at all or don't use them to communicate key messages.

Newsletters or journals do not always need to be costly, full-colour, printed publications. Provided the message is well presented in clear, easily understood language, most people will take an interest and read them. They can, however, easily be ignored or, as we found out in one organisation with a number of locations, be left in a corner, undistributed by unimpressed managers.

Some organisations have used, with great effect, pay-packets or envelopes for sending out pay statements as a means of getting messages to employees, especially those based at isolated and remote locations.

Videos

This method can obviously be costly but a number of organisations have chosen to use it to get the message across. As mentioned in Chapter 2, it offers a chance for senior management in extremely large organisations to be seen and, critically, to be seen to be putting the message across personally.

When they found that the in-house journal was not getting to the people, the senior management in the organisation referred to above decided to produce a monthly video to put across key messages. To ensure that it was effective and that all the workforce saw it, they trained their managers to 'present' it during monthly meetings. Feedback was sought and subsequently acted upon. One set of feedback led to the message in the video and the language used being simplified, but the overriding message from 'the viewers' was that the video was appreciated.

Company events, conferences, etc

A number of organisations use annual events to get messages across. These are usually in addition to other methods. The management in some organisations hold events where a 'state of the nation' type of message is presented. If the organisation is too big to make the presentation to everyone at the same time, a series of presentations, or in the case of very dispersed organisations 'road shows', have been held. In some organisations these events are held to coincide with the business planning process. At the event the previous year's performance is reviewed and the next year's plan launched.

We have found a number of organisations that have annual events off-site but these tend in the main to be smaller organisations. However, one larger organisation, Raflatac based in Scarborough, went as far as holding a conference to which all 230 employees, including those based in Stevenage and Dublin, were invited. As well as reviewing how the company had developed over the previous seven to eight years, a customer was invited to make a presentation of his views of the company's service and quality. It ended with a session where the senior management team sat on stage and answered questions from the floor.

Communication skills needed by managers

To carry out the roles mentioned above, managers need the following communication skills:
- presentational skills
- questioning skills
- chairing meetings
- listening skills
- clarifying to check understanding.

Communication, managers and the trade unions

We have found that, where organisations are committed to Investors in People and recognise trade unions, the relationship between management and unions is frequently quite cooperative. Good communication processes exist to keep the unions informed of achievements against plans and future developments, often at an early stage. Many organisations have involved the trade unions in the Investors in People process, usually through involvement in working groups.

Generally, relationships with trade unions are managed by senior staff unless organisations are very big and geographically dispersed, where local arrangements are made involving local managers.

Some organisations which do not recognise trade unions use Staff Representative Committees to consult or canvass for staff opinions and pass on information to employees. Members of these committees are often elected or nominated by their colleagues. They are expected to consult their colleagues before attending the meetings, so they do need to have some advance warning of the issues to be discussed in order to seek views.

These types of committees may serve as Works Councils for those companies which need to meet EU legislative requirements.

Summary

This chapter has examined communication as a process. It has considered why communication with the workforce is needed and how it reinforces commitment from the top to train and develop the workforce. It has detailed the methods used by some organisations and the role of managers and the skills they need.

What do managers need to do?

- Keep people informed about what the organisation is trying to achieve and their contribution.
- Keep people informed about how well the organisation is doing.
- Listen to concerns from employees and pass them back up to senior managers.
- Continually reinforce the above messages.
- Demonstrate commitment to people and their development.

THE RELEVANT INVESTORS IN PEOPLE INDICATORS

1.1 The commitment from top management to train and develop employees is communicated effectively throughout the organisation.

1.2 Employees at all levels are aware of the broad aims or vision of the organisation.

1.3 The employer has considered what employees at all levels will contribute to the success of the organisation, and has communicated this effectively to them.

1.4 Where representative structures exist, communication takes place between management and representatives on the vision of where the organisation is going and the contribution that employees (and their representatives) will make to its success.

2.5 Responsibility for training and developing employees is clearly identified and understood throughout the organisation, starting at the top.

3.4 All employees are made aware of the training and development opportunities open to them.

3.5 All employees are encouraged to help identify and meet their job-related training and development needs.

4.6 Top management's continuing commitment to training and developing employees is demonstrated to all employees.

---

5 Identifying Training and Development Needs

This chapter is essential reading for all managers as it relates to a vital stage in managing the development of people and is key to whether an organisation will meet the requirements of Investors in People. The chapter examines the involvement of the manager in the identification of training and development needs of individuals and of their team. It starts off by examining the extended training cycle. Next it looks at a number of methods used to identify training and development needs. It then examines planning for evaluation through the setting of objectives, targets and standards for training and development actions.

The (extended) training and development cycle

The first issue in managing the process is to have a helpful framework or structure. Within the Investors in People Standard there are a number of frameworks made up by linking the indicators (see Appendix 1 for the full list of indicators). For the purpose of managing the training and development process we have called this 'the extended training and development cycle' (see Figure 5.1).

Identifying individual training and development needs

In the previous chapter, as part of the communication model we addressed the issue of identifying broad aims and setting plans. This issue was also described in Chapter 3 when the role of senior

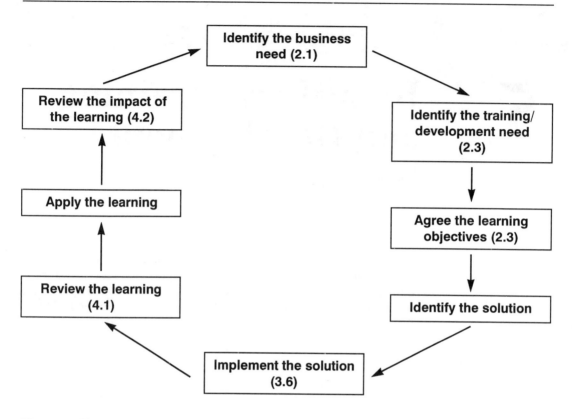

Figure 5.1 *The extended training and development cycle*

managers was discussed. This of course sets the context for the next stage in the training cycle: identifying individual and team training and development needs.

Appraisal

The most commonly used method of identifying individual training needs is through an appraisal. An effective appraisal process should offer the opportunity to review what has happened since the previous appraisal, ie, were agreed objectives met, but more importantly look ahead to the next period by agreeing what is expected of the appraisee leading to the agreement on the next set of objectives, including training and development objectives.

We agree with the usual comments concerning appraisal:

- it should be motivational;
- it should formalise what good managers have been informally doing throughout the period, such as monitoring of work, coaching and giving feedback as required; therefore there should be no surprises;
- it should allow the appraisee the opportunity to have their say, including commenting on their feelings.

Appraisal is an opportunity to communicate and reinforce the vision and mission of the organisation and clarify how the individual contributes to its success. These also set the context for the appraisal itself as in most organisations training and development should be focused on helping to meet the business objectives.

However, we do have concerns about appraisal as a vehicle for identifying training and development needs. In practice what often happens is that one or two questions are added to the end of the appraisal such as: 'Do you feel you have any training needs?', 'What training would you like?' This leads to the delivery of training and development relating to what people think they want rather than what they and their manager agree they need and inevitably leads to what is commonly referred to as a 'wish list' (ie, training activities that have little relevance to helping the organisation achieve its objectives). We return to this issue later in this chapter.

In some organisations the appraisal process is often very complicated and time-consuming and is therefore seen by managers as a chore. If managers see it in this light they are likely to approach it with an inappropriate attitude and probably will not recognise that it is a process which should be beneficial to them as well as the appraisee. It is inevitable that the appraisal process will come into disrepute in these circumstances.

In many organisations appraisals are linked to performance and therefore to pay or merit bonus. In the civil service, in spite of many attempts to separate the issues, they were linked to promotability. These issues tend to distract both the appraiser and the appraisee from the opportunity to have a meaningful discussion about training and development needs.

Finally, we have concerns about the effectiveness of training for appraisers which often concentrates on the appraisal *process* rather than the *skills* needed to carry it out effectively.

Training and development reviews

In some organisations the 'A' word – appraisal – is not well received.

The Investors in People standard does not require organisations to have an appraisal process; rather it requires a 'regular process to identify training and development needs'.

Many organisations choose, for differing reasons, to introduce a process of training and development reviews. They have many different names but essentially they carry out a similar function – to help managers identify the training and development needed to enable the individual to carry out their role.

The process is usually kept as simple as possible and consists of a short one-to-one interview which focuses on the skills and knowledge the person needs to carry out the job and whether there is a need for further development of those skills and knowledge. Some organisations may offer development opportunities beyond the needs of the individual's job in the belief that any type of development will have a spin-off on the motivation of the individual. This sometimes may get the person back into the habit of learning which can subsequently encourage the desire to develop in the workplace.

On some occasions it may not be practical to carry out one-to-one interviews. Some organisations have decided to carry out group training and development reviews. While this is not ideal it can work when the groups of people are carrying out very similar roles and provided the process offers an opportunity for people to discuss their *individual* needs, in private if necessary.

Job analysis, standards, competences, etc

Appraising or assessing training and development needs raises the issue of against what the manager assesses them. Many organisations use job analyses, others have standards and/or competences.

While the concept of job analysis is not new, the issue of competence is. When organisations have used the concept of job analysis in the past it has usually been led by training departments. Today, managers are increasingly becoming more involved in the use of these processes. The concept involves breaking down jobs into simple stages or tasks. Each stage is written down with the various actions that have to be undertaken. When a person is trained to do the job, the analysis can be used by the trainer as a 'script' to ensure that the person is trained properly and given to the trainee as an *aide mémoire*.

A number of organisations, as part of their approach to quality (often linked to ISO 9000), have included job analyses in their quality manuals, sometimes in the form of checklists. As part of the quality procedures trainees have to be 'signed off' as being able to complete the job satisfactorily. An extract from a sample checklist is included in Figure 5.2.

The concept of competence takes this a stage further. Increasingly, organisations are considering the use of National Vocational Qualifications (NVQs) as a method of assessing the competence of existing employees or developing new skills and then assessing the competence. Although some people would criticise NVQs as being bureaucratic and sometimes too broad, the competences and standards within the NVQs, which are described as performance criteria, can be used in a variety of ways and in particular to identify training and development needs.

A number of organisations which have used NVQs have trained their managers as assessors, which has had a spin-off in developing their people management skills too. Needless to say there are NVQs for assessors. (For those who are interested in finding out more about NVQs, see Appendix 2, Sources of help – NCVQ.)

NVQs have also been developed for managers. At the time of writing, these standards are being revised. For up-to-date information contact the Management Charter Initiative office (see Appendix 2). They also produce material about the relevance of the management standards to organisations working towards Investors in People status.

Personal development plans

As an outcome of appraisal or training reviews some organisations, or sometimes managers within organisations, encourage employees to draw up a personal development plan, sometimes called 'individual development plans'. Personal development plans come in a range of formats but basically they comprise written documentation that highlights what actions have been agreed at the appraisal/review. They can be very elaborate or kept very simple. At their simplest they would include:

- the purpose of the training or development action(s);
- the objectives of the action(s);
- the methodology to be used to meet the action(s);
- the date by which the action(s) should be started;
- the date by which the outcome from the action(s) should be reviewed, ie, were objectives met?

SAFE WORKING PROCEDURE

Area: Slab Grinding Bay

Activity: Abrasive Wheel Mounting

Hazards: Restricted space; Heat from wheel stub

Protective equipment required:
                     Safety helmet and boots,
                     gloves, safety jacket and trousers

Equipment required:
                     Wheel change device; torque wrench; hand hammer
                     Pneumatic spanner and socket; wooden wedges

Methodology:

Main wheel (two-man job)

	Assessed as satisfactory	
	Yes	No

1. Set machine in correct position, head back until wheel centrally over track.

2. Isolate machine, release air pressure to wheel head, switch on power to wheel change device.

3. Wedge wheel collet with wooden wedges to prevent it turning and slacken all 8 wheel bolts with torque wrench.

4. Run bolts loose with pneumatic spanner, remove and take out wedges.

5. Locate wheel change device on to central collect and lock. Withdraw and lower collet. Lift off old stub manually and discard. (Dropping stub may damage table ropes.)

6. Clean round wheel periphery to remove swarf, etc. Check explosion guard in good condition and safe.

7. Place new wheel on wheel stand. Fit new packings to front and rear of collet and locate collet on to new wheel. Turn over locking bars to secure wheel changing device.

8. Lift wheel and manipulate into position. Slide wheel into collet and when fully home secure with one stud.

9. Release locking bars, release collet securing lock and withdraw wheel changing device and return to its original position.

(Adapted from SMACC, Avesta Sheffield, Unit Trainer)

Figure 5.2 *A sample checklist*

Ideally the plans should include long-, medium- and short-term objectives but this may vary depending on the complexity of the person's job.

An example of a personal development plan for a manager is included in Figure 5.3.

Identifying team training and development needs

The most frequently used method of identifying the training and development needs of teams is the training matrix. Investors in People assessors are often presented with a training matrix as a method of identifying individual needs but unless they are very sophisticated (and therefore complex) they usually don't address the needs of individuals.

The most common reason for their use is that managers can see at a glance whether they have sufficient people trained in the range of tasks for which their team is responsible. An example of a training matrix is shown in Figure 5.4.

Purpose	Objectives	Methodology	Action from	Reviewed by
To be able to chair team meetings	To develop 'facilitation' skills – listening skills – controlling the meeting – summarising skills	1. Attendance on chairing meetings course 2. Shadow manager at regional meetings 3. Observation and feedback by manager	January February Throughout March	February End of February April
To create more time to 'supervise' the team	To develop time manage-ment systems	Attend time management module	March	End of March
	To identify tasks that can be delegated	Coaching from manager	Throughout April	Early May
To improve written reports so that report writing can be delegated by manager	To develop planning skills To be able to write in an appropriate style	Coaching and feedback from manager Review colleagues' reports for style and presentation	Middle of May Immediately	End of June Middle of May

Figure 5.3 *Example of a personal development plan*

Job \ People	Tom	Frances	Elaine	Erroll	Jagvinder	Claire
Ledger	***	**		*		
Accounts	***	***	*			
Payroll	***	*	**			
Purchasing	***	***		**		
Timesheets	***			**		
Computer:						
Word 6	**	***	*	*		***
Excel	***	**			***	
Access	*		***			***
e-mail	***	***	**	*	**	*
Post duties		***	***	*		**

Key: *** Fully trained; ** Currently being trained; * Future training need

Figure 5.4 *An example of a training matrix*

The example shows that on one axis of the matrix are listed the tasks the team have to perform and on the other a list of the people. To keep the illustration simple, the example merely shows who has been trained, who is undergoing training and who has been identified as needing training. Managers could develop the process to include symbols that show the degree of competence of the individuals and it is at this stage that they begin to address the needs of individuals.

Training matrices are of course not a new idea but quite often we have found that they are documents used by managers and kept in the manager's office, and employees never see them. What Investors in People has done has challenged this communications issue. Why should they be kept hidden away? Why shouldn't the team have the opportunity to be involved in the development of the matrix? Where team members are involved in the process they become more motivated and more willing to learn new tasks because they can see why it is necessary. They may also understand better why some training they have asked for as an individual is unlikely to take place as they can see that there are sufficient people trained to do the task to meet the needs of the team. They may not like it but they can understand it!

The manager's role versus the role of training specialists

Chapter 1 noted that in most organisations managers have the responsibility to identify training and development needs and are supported by the training specialist(s), where they exist. The processes listed above need to be kept as simple as possible if managers are to use them.

Investors in People assessors will not expect managers to be experts in training and development, but they will expect them to have a broad awareness of and use some of the various management tools that are available to help them, so that they can fulfil their responsibilities. That is why we have consistently said that where training specialists exist, they are there to *support* managers, *not to replace* them or their functions. This support can be offered in many ways:

- to help managers develop an awareness of and perhaps develop the tools and techniques that are needed to identify needs;
- to help carry out the identification of needs where a more detailed analysis is needed;
- to provide information or direct to sources of information where necessary, eg, training providers, course information, college prospectus;
- to deliver training;
- to advise and perhaps set up evaluation systems to help managers assess the effectiveness of the training.

Planning for evaluation of training and development

As evaluation is often seen as the most difficult part of becoming an Investor in People, it is important to plan.

As indicated in the extended training cycle, planning for evaluation of training and development starts with the organisation's need or objectives:

- What is the organisation trying to achieve?
- What skills or knowledge do people need to help the organisation achieve its objective?

- What skills or knowledge do people already have?
- Is there a gap between what is needed and what people already have?
- What do people therefore need to learn to be able to do?
- How will you know that they can do it?

An illustration may help clarify. The *organisational need* is to increase efficiency and therefore profitability. One method of doing this may be to increase the flexibility of the workforce. An examination of current working practice shows that most people are only able to do one job effectively. They do not support each other at times of pressure; in fact some people can be standing around while others are working flat out. You know that this needs to change.

You will *know that you have achieved this change* when all people are able to carry out at least two functions and people automatically help one another out when under pressure.

The people therefore need to learn extra knowledge and skills and teams need to be built.

Going through this process makes it easier to develop objectives.

Setting and agreeing objectives, targets and standards for training and development activities

If you don't know what you want, how can you know when you've got it?

Investors in People assessors often find that organisations and their managers have difficulties with evaluation because they are poor at objective setting.

We have found that poorly constructed training and development objectives are usually vague. Vague objectives are usually not objectives at all, but aims, ie, broad statements of what is required.

One example of a vague objective we found concerned training for a receptionist where the objective that had been agreed was: '*to improve reception skills*'. A course had been identified and the person was ready to go. When the manager of the receptionist was asked how she would know when the receptionist's skills had improved, the answer at first was as vague as the objective. However, with further probing it transpired that the receptionist did not have a weakness in the skills needed in dealing with customers (the subject of the course) either by phone or in person; rather she was unable to answer the questions posed by customers. She constantly had to consult other people for information which did not look very professional to customers and caused interruptions for the people she consulted. The need was not for improved reception skills but for increased knowledge about the organisation and its services. Therefore the manager would know that the training need had been addressed when the receptionist's knowledge had increased and she was more self-sufficient. The training course was cancelled and internal arrangements were made to increase the person's knowledge.

This may seem an extreme example but it is a true one. It raises the question, if objectives are not clarified, how often do people go on the wrong course? Setting the criteria for learning in advance is very important. Some of the issues to consider are shown in Figure 5.5.

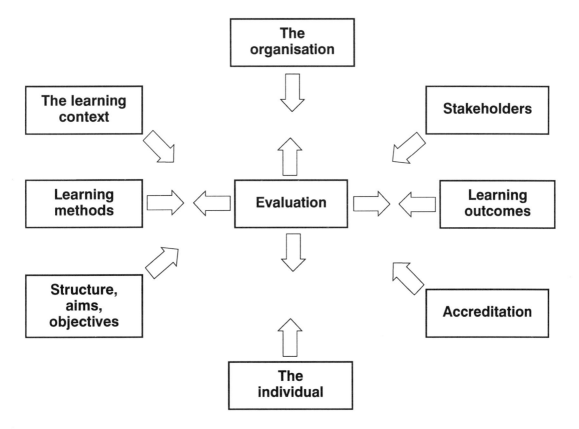

Figure 5.5 *Setting criteria*

Sometimes objectives may exist in the minds of the people concerned but are not written down, discussed and agreed. While it may be acceptable to agree objectives verbally, there is less room for misunderstanding if they are written down. When it comes to evaluating whether the objectives have been achieved, it is also much easier to check if they are in writing.

Objectives can be made clearer and more specific by simply asking the question, 'How will I know when the person demonstrates the new skill or applies the newly acquired knowledge?'

Training specialists often refer to 'SMART' objectives. The initials stand for:

- Specific
- Measurable
- Achievable
- Realistic and
- Timebound.

An example of a SMART objective for training the receptionist mentioned above would be:

'By the end of the training session, the receptionist would to be able to demonstrate that she has the knowledge to answer ten questions on the five main services offered by the organisation.'

To illustrate further, there are examples of aims and objectives for a workshop on the subject of this book given in Figure 5.6.

To be even more specific and therefore make objectives more measurable, targets and standards can be built into the objectives.

Targets normally refer to *quantity* eg, 'to be able to make 50 widgets an hour' or 'to type at 50 words per minute'.

Standards normally refer to *quality* eg, 'to be able to produce financial forecasts to 100% accuracy' or 'to be able to produce widgets to tolerances of 0.01 cm'.

Standards are often defined by customers and, as mentioned earlier in this chapter, organisations with quality procedures usually write the quality standards into the quality manual. The checklists also mentioned earlier (see Figure 5.2) will probably include standards which determine whether a person is competent or not. When it comes to written work, most organisations have a house style or corporate image – another type of standard.

Value statements, customer charters, perhaps even mission statements, may define organisational standards. However, when it comes

INVESTORS IN PEOPLE WORKSHOP

THE LINE MANAGER'S ROLE
IN INVESTORS IN PEOPLE

Aim:

To ensure line managers understand the role an assessor will expect them to play in helping the organisation to achieve the Investors in People Standard.

Objectives:

By the end of the workshop participants will:

(a) Understand which indicators their actions affect and how they can help the organisation meet the Standard.

(b) Have increased their understanding of the Investors in People Standard and its indicators.

(c) Understand what 'development' is in an Investors in People context.

(d) Have identified any barriers that may stop them carrying out the role required.

(e) If there are barriers they will have identified methods of overcoming them.

Figure 5.6 *Example of a workshop's aims and objectives*

to personal standards it becomes more difficult. Managers will also have their own standards and unfortunately these may vary from one manager to another. It is therefore important that managers clearly communicate what their standards are. Some managers are frequently dissatisfied with work produced by members of staff – this is often because they have not defined what they expect, ie, the standard. Personal standards are often difficult to describe. For example, in written work it may be as simple as having certain phrases or words that they would like their staff not to use.

Communication, coaching and feedback are the keys to ensuring that employees know what the standards are and are trained to deliver to those standards. Part of the manager's role prior to training is therefore to have a discussion to ensure that the person knows why they are undertaking the training, and to clarify that what the manager expects the person to be able to do following the event is the same as the trainee's expectations. This briefing may be quite short in some cases, but ideally a note should be kept so that it can be referred to for evaluation after the event. Some organisations have produced a form (see Appendix 3), the first page of which can be used for this pre-event discussion.

Summary

This chapter has examined the actions a manager would be expected to carry out in order to identify the training and development needs of individuals and their teams. It has included a model – the extended training cycle – and some examples of the methods used by some organisations. Finally, it has examined setting objectives for training and development activities.

What do managers need to do?

- Be aware of the needs of the organisation.
- Carry out regular reviews of the training and development needs of their people in order that they are able to meet their performance objectives.
- Agree SMART objectives for training and developmental or *learning* activity before the activity takes place.

THE RELEVANT INVESTORS IN PEOPLE INDICATORS

1.2 Employees at all levels are aware of the broad aims or vision of the organisation.

1.3 The employer has considered what employees at all levels will contribute to the success of the organisation, and has communicated this effectively to them.

2.3 Training and development needs are regularly reviewed against goals and targets at the organisation, team and individual level.

2.5 Responsibility for training and developing employees is clearly identified and understood throughout the organisation, starting at the top.

2.6 Objectives are set for training and development actions at the organisation, team and individual level.

3.2 Managers are effective in carrying out their responsibilities for training and developing employees.

3.3 Managers are actively involved in supporting employees to meet their training and development needs.

3.4 All employees are made aware of the training and development opportunities open to them.

3.5 All employees are encouraged to help identify and meet their job-related training and development needs.

4.1 The organisation evaluates the impact of training and development actions on knowledge, skills and attitude.

4.2 The organisation evaluates the impact of training and development actions on performance.

6 Identifying Solutions

Throughout this book we have very rarely mentioned training without also mentioning development. The Investors in People indicators also couple training and development. Identifying training solutions is fairly straightforward in most organisations so this chapter is concentrating on development. It starts by looking at what it is and looks at some of the vast range of methods available to managers to develop their people.

Definition

The *Oxford English Dictionary* defines 'develop' as: 'to make or become larger or fuller or more mature or organised'. In the context of developing *people* there are many definitions. The definition we include uses words with a similar meaning to those in the above dictionary definition: 'To broaden and enhance the skills, knowledge and attitudes of groups and individuals in order to maximise potential'.

The key words in this definition are *broaden, enhance* and *maximise potential*. These suggest that the act of developing people is to build on something that is already there. It is difficult, and perhaps unnecessary, to define the difference between training and development because they overlap so much. However, it is important to acknowledge that *all training is development but not all development is training*. Many managers tend to focus on training courses when faced with the need to help people develop skills. To some it may be the easy option but it may not be the most appropriate or the one with the greatest potential for success. To help managers consider what other options they have, this chapter concentrates on those aspects of development which are not training.

Another way to look at development is to look at it as 'learning'. In *Investors in People Explained* (Taylor and Thackwray, 1996) we considered learning organisations and their relationship to Investors in People. Development is an integral part of the activity of a learning organisation.

Development should involve stretching people to test out their potential. For people with lots of potential and/or ambition, this may involve a huge 'stretch'; for others it may simply be a short step. It may involve asking them to do something new; it may be merely building on something they already do.

Planning for development

Whatever the reason, development should be planned and structured. Inevitably, unplanned development opportunities will occur and it would be foolish not to take them up.

As with training, planned development should have a purpose, eg, to take on new or different responsibilities in order to test potential or encourage creativeness. It should have SMART objectives, as described in Chapter 5, and it should be structured. One way of giving it structure is to make it a 'development programme' or 'project'. This will be a series of linked activities each supporting or building on one another. For example, an induction programme is a development 'programme' with the purpose of introducing new staff to the organisation (and the organisation to the new staff), its people and the individual's work. Induction often includes a training event as part of the 'programme'; so too could other types of development programme.

As described in Chapter 5, those being developed should be briefed prior to commencing the programme and the purpose and objectives agreed. Because some development projects may be spread over a period of time, plans to monitor progress should be agreed, with review dates entered in diaries.

To some managers this may appear to involve extra work. For some it may, but for many a lot of processes will already exist and may merely need refining. In Chapter 5 we referred to a variety of methods of identifying needs – appraisal, training and development reviews and personal development plans. These are all vehicles to enable the manager to 'manage' development. However, in many organisations we have found that these processes concentrate on the traditional methods, ie, training courses, rather than considering alternative methods.

So what are the alternative methods?

Development activities

When reading the following section, many will find themselves saying, 'We do many of these things, so what's new?' Perhaps nothing, but could it be more structured? Can you evaluate its impact? (Chapter 8 will look at evaluating development.)

Reading

Most people will read and will 'learn'. For many people the only way of keeping up to date with the latest trends and ideas within their professions is to read newspapers, books, journals, etc. For others reading reports is part of their job and for some, such as researchers perhaps, reading may be a large part of their job. Some people don't find the time to read while others may find the thought of having to read to learn off-putting as it is not their preferred style of learning. However, there is no doubt that reading is developmental and should be considered as one of the options when putting together a developmental programme.

Open learning

For those who do not like reading perhaps open learning (sometimes referred to as distance or flexible learning) offers a more attractive alternative. There is a huge variety of open learning methodologies (reading itself is one) so we are concentrating on some of the most popular ones.

First there are audio and video tapes. Audio tapes are quite a useful and perhaps less time-consuming method as they could be played while driving; however, this does present difficulties if you want to make a note of key points.

There are a variety of computer-based training methods including tutorials that come with software packages, CD-ROM interactive packages, etc. There are also still in use programme textbooks in some organisations but these have generally been replaced by computer-based packages.

Discovery learning

Some people learn how to use computer software packages by this method – trial and error, trying out different commands to see what happens. For people who have a basic knowledge, perhaps those who have been on a training course, it is quite an appropriate method as computer packages are so complex, a training event cannot possibly cover all aspects. The same principles can be used in other ways. Some organisations use discovery learning as a method of induction – researching and interviewing people to learn about the organisation. An advantage of discovery learning is the fact that people are not being 'taught' but are 'learning' and are therefore more likely to retain the information or skills.

Observing, questioning, thinking, reviewing mistakes, etc

These to a large extent go hand in glove with discovery learning. Watching other people is probably the most common method of self-development; we do it all the time, but do we always think about it sufficiently and review what we've seen? This of course is especially important in the workplace because a lot of learning can take place by observing role models. However to *understand* why people have done things in certain ways, or perhaps *not* done it in a certain way, it is necessary to ask questions.

It is often said that people are their own harshest critics. This is often because we know we could have done better. Sometimes we may feel this way even though everyone else said we did OK! Reflecting on what went well and what didn't go so well is a very powerful developmental tool provided notes are kept, either mentally or in writing.

Shadowing, attachments, secondments, etc

These methods follow on from above. They can be long-term approaches, eg, six-month secondments, or short. They can have many different purposes, from widening knowledge and experience to learning how customers think.

Visits

A visit could be classed as an extremely short attachment. Visits as developmental opportunities appeared to fall into disuse for a while, but we have found that their use is increasing. They are often incorporated into Total Quality strategies when visits are used for people from various parts of the organisation to get to know customers, or help people understand what happens to their product once it leaves them. In the service sector they may be used as a method of finding out the best practice by observing what competitors are doing. If organisations are large and/or geographically dispersed, visits will serve to build teams and relationships. It is often helpful for administrators or shop-floor workers to go out with sales reps on sales visits, or for administrators to visit the shop floor.

Attendance at conferences, exhibitions, etc

These of course are another type of 'visit'. Many organisations encourage their people to attend this type of event to look at the latest ideas and technology, among other things. Quite often the purpose may be obvious, but are the outcomes always evaluated? Could they be more structured? If more than one person attends, is there duplication of effort? Some organisations only send senior people to such events. Would there be a benefit in sending more junior people or shop-floor workers?

In some organisations there is a reluctance by some managers to encourage visits whether they be to other organisations or exhibitions. This is frequently because the managers simply don't trust their people to make full use of the visit for its intended purpose. Of course such activities could be open to abuse, but if the culture of the organisation is one that encourages development or learning the vast majority of people do not abuse these opportunities. Other managers say it's a perk. Of course visits are perks but people can learn from them and many managers find that when people return they apply what they've learnt. They are also often more motivated and frequently work harder to make up for the production time they lost.

Job swaps

Rather than just visit other parts of the organisation, why not swap jobs for a short time? A good illustration of how useful this can be occurred in a company mentioned earlier: Raflatac. As part of a number of development initiatives, managers encouraged job swaps and as a result a member of the dispatch team ended up working in the sales office. He received a phone call from a customer complaining about the non-receipt of an urgent item. Apparently the previous night, as it was getting late, he had put aside the parcel 'as another day would not make a difference'. After dealing with the complaint he realised it did make a difference. This illustrates how job swaps help people understand the implications of their actions, or non-actions, and can lead to improvements in the quality of service.

Delegation

The correct use of delegation as a management tool should lead to lots of developmental opportunities. It can combine some of the benefits of job swaps, such as understanding the manager's role, with the opportunity to make people's jobs more interesting. Effective delegation involves a number of simple steps:

- correct identification of the task to be delegated, eg, not high risk;
- correct identification of the person to whom work is being delegated – are they capable? Are they willing?
- briefing and coaching to ensure they know what they are expected to do, how to do it and what to do if they need help;
- monitor how they are doing but not too closely. If you can't trust them to get on with it you've probably chosen the wrong person;
- be available if required;
- review what has been learnt.

Job rotation, rotating duties

Whereas delegation most likely involves the manager passing work down to staff, job rotation involves people doing other jobs at the same level. This can be particularly useful in areas where jobs are perhaps straightforward and rather boring, and people need motivating. Rotating duties is similar, but may be simply encouraging people to rotate who takes the minutes of meetings. It could include aspects of delegation and the manager could rotate who chairs the meeting. The guidelines for delegation should be followed.

Attending meetings, sharing information/ideas/good practice, etc

As most people attend meetings at some time or other they are another developmental opportunity that readers may consider obvious. Not every meeting will be a learning opportunity but, as mentioned above in relation to thinking, it is how the learning is assessed and used that is important.

Quality circles/improvement groups

While some organisations may consider quality circles a bit old fashioned, many use a variant of them, often referred to as 'continuous improvement groups'. They are used in a variety of ways, sometimes to solve problems, sometimes to generate new ideas and improve systems, etc as part of quality initiatives. They can involve a variety of methodologies such as brainstorming. Sometimes the 'learning' is difficult to assess as it is integrated with the improvements to processes, products and other improvements.

Some organisations empower their people to run and manage these types of groups and only involve managers when it is essential. These groups can therefore offer alternative development opportunities: to develop the skills associated with setting up groups, agreeing and circulating agendas, managing and/or chairing the groups, etc.

Special projects

In some organisations some improvement groups may be viewed as special projects, while in others the outcome may be to set up a project or pilot. Some projects may involve groups of people; others may just involve one person. They may form part of the action associated with another learning or development opportunity. They may be associated with a qualification such as an MBA.

Once again evaluating the 'learning' from a project may not always be easy, but if it is planned properly it will have an evaluation strategy and it may be simple to set 'learning objectives' as part of the overall project plan.

Is there another way?

This question is usually associated with the Japanese approach known as '*Kaizen*' – the search for a better way. Quality circles or improvement groups are one approach; there are others. They don't need to be complex. The traditional staff suggestion scheme is one method. Other organisations encourage people to innovate, experiment or simply do something in a different way. Being creative and imaginative, turning things on their head, can all lead to lots of new ideas and approaches and involve lots of 'learning'. One example is HPC in Stevenage, Herts. It operates a scheme which promotes training and development activities beyond those that relate to business objectives as part of its commitment to lifelong learning. Following a recommendation from a colleague for helping/assisting with something 'above and beyond the call of duty', or for contributing to the in-house journal, points are awarded to a certain value. The tokens are exchangeable only for training and development activities.

Self-development

People, of course, should not need to wait for their managers to identify the need for development. All the above are options for people to chose for their own development, whether work related or not. Organisations which have, or are developing, a learning culture will create a climate whereby people *want* to learn and develop. Some organisations have been working towards developing this culture for some time. The Rover Group, for example, has set up a separate business, 'The Rover Learning Business', to help manage and provide opportunities for the development of employees.

Self-development sits comfortably with 'lifelong learning' which is a concept being promoted to encourage people to develop skills and knowledge in order to help them compete in what is often seen as a less secure working environment.

Personal development

Although everything mentioned above could be classed as personal development, it is largely development that is related to the needs of the person's organisation. Personal development is clearly much wider than this. In these days of tight budgets, many organisations only support development which will lead to business benefits. There are, however, a number of organisations which do support more or less any kind of development activity as they believe it will encourage a learning climate. The Ford Motor Company has long had such a programme but it is not just large organisations which promote such schemes. Raflatac, which has been mentioned a number of times in this book, offers each of its employees £50 per year to spend as they wish on development. The original idea was that it should be used for college fees, but in practice it has been used in many different ways, eg, on driving lessons. To promote this concept, Sheffield Training Enterprise Council has introduced a local programme, 'Employee Led Development' (ELD) which offers matched funding to employers in Sheffield who are prepared to support non-business-related development for their employees.

Summary

This chapter has looked at where development fits in. It has attempted to define what development is and how it relates to the concept of a 'learning organisation'. It has examined a selection of developmental activities and ended by looking at self-development and personal development.

What do managers need to do?

- Be clear on the organisation's policy in terms of supporting development.
- Encourage employees by creating a 'learning climate'.
- Keep people informed about developmental opportunities, or be able to direct their employees to the source of such information.
- Support and encourage those employees who take up developmental opportunities.

Reference

Taylor, P and Thackwray, R (1996) *Investors in People Explained*, 2nd edn, London: Kogan Page.

RELEVANT INVESTORS IN PEOPLE INDICATORS

1.1 The commitment from top management to train and develop employees is communicated effectively throughout the organisation.

2.2 A written plan identifies the organisation's training and development needs, and specifies what action will be taken to meet these needs.

2.3 Training and development needs are regularly reviewed against goals and targets at the organisation, team and individual level.

2.4 A written plan identifies the resources that will be used to meet training and development needs.

2.6 Objectives are set for training and development actions at the organisation, team and individual level.

2.7 Where appropriate, training and development needs are linked to external standards such as National Vocational Qualifications (NVQs) or Scottish Vocational Qualifications (SVQs) and units.

3.1 All new employees are introduced effectively to the organisation and all employees new to a job are given the training and development they need to do that job.

3.2 Managers are effective in carrying out their responsibilities for training and developing employees.

3.3 Managers are actively involved in supporting employees to meet their training and development needs.

3.4 All employees are made aware of the training and development opportunities open to them.

3.5 All employees are encouraged to help identify and meet their job-related training and development needs.

3.6 Action takes place to meet the training and development needs of individuals, teams and the organisation.

4.6 Top management's continuing commitment to training and developing employees is demonstrated to all employees.

7 Implementing the Solutions

This is probably one of the most important chapters in the book because it is about what managers, supervisors etc, should actually *do*. We therefore go into more detail about some of the issues which managers need to be aware of in order to be effective.

One of the Investors in People indicators (3.3) states that: 'managers are actively involved in supporting employees to meet their training and development needs'. It does not mean that managers have do *everything* but it does mean they have to do *something*.

Active support starts before the training and development activity and continues during and after it. Here we build on the previous chapters which concerned active support prior to the training and development activity. This chapter focuses on implementing the identified training and development solutions.

It examines what managers should do to actively support employees through the activity. It starts by looking at induction for new employees and goes on to look at coaching and feedback. It links to Chapter 8 which examines the active support following training through evaluation.

Induction

Why bother?

Research has shown that the first few days and weeks are critical to the opinions formed by new employees of their new employer. Organisations which lose new employees quickly, even those 'grateful' for a job, inevitably lose them because the organisation has not met their expectations. The costs of recruiting and selecting new employees are high not only in terms of time and money but in disruption too. Anything that can be done to minimise this must be very welcome; induction should be a significant factor here.

Eight benefits of an effective induction

New starters will:

1. Be able to explain the organisation's mission and aims and see where their jobs fit in.
2. Know that the organisation is committed to training and developing its employees and of future opportunities that may exist.
3. Be more likely to remain with the organisation thus reducing employment costs by reducing labour turnover.
4. Be more motivated and able to be more effective – sooner.
5. Be aware of the need to promote quality or other key organisational values.
6. Build links with existing employees (eg, through mentoring/ coaching schemes).
7. Be aware of the legal requirements and organisational policies on health and safety, equal opportunities, etc.
8. Be aware of organisational messages before getting locked into departmental or sectional loyalties.

What is induction?

The Arbitration, Conciliation and Advisory Service (ACAS) guidelines define induction as 'helping a new employee to settle down into a new job as soon as possible, by becoming familiar with the people, surroundings, job, and the firm and industry'.

Most people can recall how they have experienced poor induction and many people may feel that it is a thing of the past; we have found that this is not the case. We have found that new starters are sometimes dropped in at the deep end with little information while others are overloaded with information about the organisation and are introduced to *everybody* and everything. When it does take place, induction is often unstructured and poorly planned and may take little account of past experience. Induction, or the introduction to the new organisation, starts at recruitment. As the personnel role is devolved to managers they are becoming involved at the selection and interviewing stages. Some organisations, such as Hewlett Packard, encourage managers to contact new appointees before they start work so that the process of 'joining' the new organisation starts early.

Induction courses, packs, etc

In many organisations induction is often seen as the 'induction course' or 'pack' that is presented to the new person on the first day. The problem with having induction courses is that they rely on having sufficient new starters to ensure courses are run frequently and are viable. In many organisations this is not the case and there are examples of people going on the induction course six months or even longer after they have started. The value of the course is lost and the person is probably not very motivated by such late induction no matter how valuable some parts of the course may be.

Courses also suggest that induction is a one-off event when it should be seen as a continuing process. Graduate entry programmes are induction programmes and may last for a year or more.

To overcome the problem of courses that are infrequent or not viable, a number of organisations have developed induction packs, a type of open learning version of the induction course, but what often happens with these packs is that they become an easy option: they are given to the new starter to work through with little guidance or support.

The line manager's role in induction

The key responsibility is to identify requirements (ie, the nature, scope, depth) and then to see that they are met. People who have never had a job before or those who have been out of the job market for some time are likely to have differing needs to those who are changing employers. These needs should be clarified and for some people a type of appraisal or training review may be appropriate. New employees, even at more senior levels, will need induction although they may have to take more responsibility for organising it themselves.

How much of the induction the manager actually delivers personally will vary from manager to manager. First-line managers will clearly be more involved than middle and senior managers. However, even very senior managers should have a role to play as induction offers an opportunity for them to demonstrate their commitment to training and development.

Active support for induction means that the manager has a role to play whether there is a course or a pack, even if initially it is only to welcome the person to the organisation. If managers delegate responsibility for delivering induction they should ensure that the inductor has the knowledge and skills to carry it out effectively. A checklist of the more common topics that should be considered by managers when designing induction programmes is given below.

Planning and delivering induction – the issues to consider for inclusion

Although local priorities and needs will vary to some extent, it is clear that there are six key areas that induction should address. They are:

1. The job
2. Personnel issues
3. The department/unit/section
4. Other departments/units/sections
5. The organisation
6. The area.

These are examined in more detail below. Clear lines of accountability should link each of these areas and their component elements to a particular function (ie, manager, colleague, mentor, personnel, other). The methodology should also be agreed (ie, mode of delivery – documents, face-to-face, visits, formal induction, other).

Line managers should ensure that all are addressed in full, either via the corporate induction programme, or local induction. The appraisal process must incorporate an opportunity for the new member of staff and his or her line manager to reflect on the contribution made to individual and departmental development by induction.

1. The job

The line manager must ensure that the new member of staff is supported in gaining knowledge of:

- duties, responsibilities, workload
- standards and expectations
- accommodation
- resources
- sources of information and support including arrangements for allocation of mentors/coaching arrangements
- useful contacts.

2. Personnel issues

The line manager must ensure that the new member of staff is supported in gaining knowledge of:

- pay and pensions
- hours and holidays
- sickness and leave

- appraisal
- promotion
- discipline, complaints and grievance procedures
- trade unions and professional associations
- staff support and counselling
- staff benefits
- financial matters.

3. The department, unit, section

The line manager must ensure that the new member of staff is supported in gaining knowledge of:

- structure and management
- plans and activities
- resources
- people
- policies and procedures
- communications
- facilities
- geography
- equipment
- health and safety
- personal and professional development opportunities (local and corporate).

4. Other departments/units/sections

The line manager must ensure that the new member of staff is supported in gaining knowledge of:

- purpose and activities
- structure
- communications
- contacts
- policies and procedures
- geography
- facilities and resources.

5. The organisation

The line manager must ensure that the new member of staff is supported in gaining knowledge of:

- history and mission
- structure and management
- planning

- funding
- activities and resources
- people
- communications
- facilities, especially parking, crèche, medical, catering, social policies and procedures, especially equal opportunities, health and safety, quality assurance, financial regulations, geography, calendar.

6. The area

The line manager must ensure that the new member of staff is supported in gaining knowledge of:

- geography
- transport
- accommodation
- facilities
- personal needs.

Alternative induction strategies

CD-ROM/interactive video

Although this may be considered a type of pack, we thought it worth highlighting as a number of larger organisations have developed their own multimedia packages that new employees can work through. Some are designed to be spread over a period of time and encourage the involvement of line managers through the setting of tests that they should review with the inductee.

Mentoring/coaching/buddy systems, etc

The mentor (or 'starter's friend' or 'buddy') is a response which should allow each new person access to the information they need, when they need it, in a form they can handle. The degree of formality adopted by different organisations varies widely, from very casual attachment to nominated trainer with responsibilities under the probationary procedures. Critical issues here include the preparation, selection and support of those staff who will act as mentors, as well as support for the (unfortunately titled) 'mentees'. This is especially crucial during the all-important first six weeks. Having a mentor or buddy who is not a manager allows the opportunity for the new starter to ask naive questions without embarrassment. In some organisations we have found that mentors can have more empathy with new starters if they are recent inductees, suitably trained of course.

'Discovery' learning

To avoid overloading new employees with too much information and to help people *learn* rather than be *told* some organisations or their managers have developed a different approach to induction. This involves the inductee having to discover information about the organisation through research or interviewing people. The new person would be briefed and pointed in the right direction then debriefed afterwards. This method offers various opportunities, especially when associated with other more traditional induction methods.

Changing job/role within the same organisation

At a number of recent events we have been involved in, a straw poll of participants showed a significant number of them felt that they had experience of being 'dropped in it' when they had changed jobs *within* organisations. It seems that some managers, at all levels within organisations, assume that people who take up a new role, whether it is through promotion or level transfer, do not need any kind of introduction or support to carry out the new job. The most dangerous thing any manager can do is assume anything. Some people say that the word assume means 'It makes an *ass* out of *u* and *me*'.

When someone changes jobs the first thing that should be carried out is a training and development review, from which a development plan can be drawn up. What happens in practice is that the appraisal or review process is often put on hold until the person has settled into the new job. We have found that some people who have changed jobs have not had an appraisal or review for 18 months or more! The line manager has a clear responsibility to ensure that this does not happen.

Existing employees

The previous chapter described the actions a manager should take prior to training and development taking place. Depending what the training and development actions are, the line manager will have certain responsibilities to carry out while they are taking place.

The first responsibility is to ensure that, when a need has been identified and objectives agreed, the action actually takes place. All too often we have found that for various reasons, but usually due to work pressures, needs are not met. If work constantly gets in the way of meeting training and development needs then the Investors in People assessor will question the commitment of either the organisation, the line manager, or both. If the training and development is *needed* then it should take place. Clearly not all needs can be met immediately but over a period of time they should be.

Managing the 'wish list'

In the previous chapter we raised the issue of appraisal identifying a 'wish list' of training and development that the individual wants rather than needs. This is a difficult job for managers but the Investors in People Standard offers a coherent framework which should help managers with this task.

Most organisations have not got unlimited resources for training and development. The focus therefore should always be on training and development that contributes to the organisation's business objectives. Whenever an employee identifies a need the manager should encourage them to say why they think it helps meet these objectives. If the process of relating training and development to business needs is constantly adopted, some of the more extreme 'needs' will not be raised. The following describes an example of a dialogue between an employer and employee to illustrate this issue.

During the course of a training review, a Domestic Assistant in a nursing home asked if she could be trained as a flower arranger. The Matron, who was carrying out the review, asked how it would help the organisation. The Domestic Assistant pointed out that it was important that the home was made pleasant and homely for residents and that prospective customers, when visiting the home, saw that this was the case. Arranging flowers contributed to this objective. The home from time to time brought in and paid a qualified flower arranger so there were potential savings if the Domestic Assistant could do it. The Matron decided that the training should take place.

Investors in People requires organisations to identify at organisational level what training and development at a broad level is required to meet business needs. This too can offer a steer to employees if it is communicated to them. When individuals create 'wish lists', we have found that it is because employees are unaware of the organisation's priorities for training and development.

Finally, if all else fails do what the Food and Beverage Manager at the Ramada Hotel, Heathrow did – present the wish list to the staff for them to decide what the priorities were.

Actively supporting

When it has been decided that the training or developmental need will be met, if the need is being met off-the-job it is unlikely that the line manager will have anything to do until the person returns. Post-training activity will be dealt with in Chapter 8.

If the need is being met on-the-job, the line manager support may entail either:

- keeping a watching brief if the training has been delegated to an on-the-job trainer; *or*
- direct coaching and/or feedback by the line manager.

Keeping a watching brief

As the line manager is responsible for training and development, even if they have delegated the delivery to another person within their team, they need to ensure that the delivery is effective. This can be done in a variety of ways but the most important is that they should ensure that the person delivering it is capable. This may mean coaching and feedback to the trainer themselves and perhaps some monitoring in the initial stages, especially if the trainer is relatively inexperienced. As with any task that is being managed, the line manager should be available to handle any difficulties that arise. Once the delivery activity is completed the manager should carry out the post-training activity.

Coaching

This is one of the most important roles a line manager has in the development of people.

The *Oxford English Dictionary* defines a coach as 'a person who trains or teaches'. We would define coaching as: 'the process by which an individual trains or teaches another person, usually on a one-to-one basis and on-the-job, through the *sharing* of skills and knowledge in order to guide them to better results'.

The coach does not always have to be a line manager but all line managers should be able to coach. Coaching is usually a process rather than an event. Although it can be spontaneous it should be planned; good coaches would constantly be watching out for opportunities to coach, but they would also ensure that it is structured.

To be a successful coach, managers should be:

- good facilitators, ie, ask questions to check knowledge and understanding rather than *tell* people how and what to do;
- good listeners
- able to use silence
- observant
- knowledgeable about the subject
- encouraging, good motivators
- credible
- willing to take risks.

The coaching process involves the following:

- spot opportunities and prepare
- check existing knowledge and understanding
- remember, tell – show – do, ie:
- *tell* – the person what you're going to do and why and what they should be able to do after the activity
- *show* – the person how to do it
- *do* – get the person to do it
- check understanding
- ask the person to do it again
- once satisfied that they can do it monitor progress, but not too closely, to avoid showing distrust.

Feedback

The ability to give feedback goes hand-in-hand with coaching skills.

The Oxford dictionary defines feedback as, 'The return of infomation to its supplier', so in a training and development context the definition could be: 'A communication process to an individual (or group) to inform them how their actions/behaviour affects others'.

The purpose of feedback is to *help* people learn/change behaviour.

When to give feedback

Feedback will often be given in formal situations, such as appraisal interviews, a training course following role plays, etc, or during coaching sessions. However, there may be times in informal situations such as a review of a meeting or presentation, when it may be appropriate to offer feedback. Both formal and informal situations involve a type of appraisal, or assessment; however, the major difference between these situation concerns the expectations of the recipient of the feedback.

In formal situations the recipient will expect to be given feedback because that is often a major part of the purpose of the situation. In informal situations, because the recipient may not expect feedback, it may be best to *offer* feedback, rather than *give* it. If the person refuses the feedback, but you feel it is important, then you may have to agree an appropriate time to give it.

Feedback and the use of competences, standards, etc

In all these situations the feedback should follow an observation and analysis of performance. This implies that the giver of the feedback should have some criteria, competence or standards against which to judge the person's performance. It is important to the receiver of the feedback that they understand in advance what these criteria are, especially in the formal situation. This links back to the job analysis, competences etc, discussed in Chapter 5.

In the informal situation, there may be times when the recipient does not know the criteria and this needs to be taken into account when offering the feedback.

Good practice

- Set the right 'climate'.
- Choose the right time, ie, not last thing at night or following a stressful event.
- Establish mutual trust between the giver and recipient. This is not always easy when you are the 'boss' and the receiver is a member of your staff.
- Handle resistance to change; as in any change situation it is likely that there could be some resistance or discomfort.
- Adopt a 'helping mode' of joint exploration.
- Ask the person *how they think they did* before telling them how you think they did. This often avoids confrontations if the person thinks they did well and you don't. If they do think they did well ask them, 'What was it that went well? What could you do differently?' This ensures that they know *why* it went well and that it was not just good luck.
- Concentrate on listening to their comments before giving feedback; most people are more critical of themselves than you

would be and they will probably give you a lead on which to build your feedback.

Some useful tips

Formula for successful feedback

1. **O**bserve the behaviour.
2. **A**nalyse the behaviour – look for strengths as well as weaknesses.
3. **F**eed back; reinforce what was good as well as areas for improvement, check the reaction and agree the desired behaviour.
4. **S**upport in order to change to the desired behaviour.

Remember **OAFS**.

Constructive feedback

1. *Descriptive rather than evaluative* – it should describe what was observed in an objective manner. Evaluative feedback is likely to be subjective.
2. *Specific rather than general* – focus on specific issues and illustrate with examples.
3. *Avoid prescription* – what works for you may not always work for another person. Try to get the person to suggest what they will do differently so that they will 'own' the change in behaviour. However, if there is only one way to do something then prescription may be the only way.
4. *Focus on modifiable behaviour* – it's no use focusing on issues that cannot be changed such as personality, stammers, etc.
5. *Well timed* – it should be given *almost* immediately. Allow time for the person to reflect on their performance. However, if it is left too long the person may not recall enough about their performance to make the feedback worthwhile.
6. *Balanced* – identifies both strengths and weaknesses. Try not to be over-critical or to praise too much. Avoiding 'overload' is important: people can only tackle so many issues at once. When there are a large number of issues it is important to focus on the appropriate or urgent ones. The other, less urgent, issues can be tackled later.
7. *Validated with the receiver* – check understanding with the recipient of the feedback. Unless you do this the recipient may not change behaviour in the expected way.

Traps to avoid

1. Starting your feedback with the words, 'If I were you...'. This usually means: 'If I were you (which I'm not)... I would do it like this (which you did not)'.
2. Giving unsolicited feedback – a lot of people like to give feedback but this is the type that is often ignored or could lead to disagreements and you enter a 'defend/attack' situation.
3. Denying a person's feelings – if people say they feel a certain way then that is the way they feel.
4. Raising irrelevant issues – eg, a person who is being coached on telephone-handling skills scratches their head or blinks a lot. It may be accurate feedback, but is it relevant?
5. Goal-centred feedback – usually describes what should have happened rather than what did happen. This type of feedback does not take account of where the person is now!
6. Allowing the person to become dependent on you – the idea of giving feedback is to enable the person to adopt the agreed behaviour. They may need some further support but not to the extent that they are reliant on you.

Summary

This chapter has examined what active support by the line manager actually involves. It has looked at support for induction processes for new employees and job changers. It has looked at supporting the needs of existing employees and how to manage the 'wish list'. Finally, it has looked at coaching and feedback skills, an important part of active support.

What do managers need to do?

- Ensure all new employees are inducted to their job.
- Identify the skills and knowledge that employees need in order to do their jobs.
- Review the skills and knowledge that employees have.
- Encourage employees to identify their own development solutions.
- Provide (or guide to) information about development opportunities, including access to qualifications as appropriate.

- Agree appropriate action to fill any gaps that employees may have in terms of skills or knowledge.
- Ensure the agreed action takes place.
- Agree desired outcomes ('learning objectives') *before* the action commences.
- Support the action as appropriate, eg, through coaching and feedback.
- Check that the action has been successful and that the new skills and knowledge can be applied.
- Check that the new skills or knowledge *are* being applied and are having the desired results.
- If not, start the above cycle again.

THE RELEVANT INVESTORS IN PEOPLE INDICATORS

1.1 The commitment from top management to train and develop employees is communicated effectively throughout the organisation.

1.2 Employees at all levels are aware of the broad aims or vision of the organisation.

1.3 The employer has considered what employees at all levels will contribute to the success of the organisation, and has communicated this effectively to them.

2.1 A written but flexible plan sets out the organisation's goals and targets.

2.2 A written plan identifies the organisation's training and development needs, and specifies what action will be taken to meet these needs.

2.3 Training and development needs are regularly reviewed against goals and targets at the organisation, team and individual level.

2.4 A written plan identifies the resources that will be used to meet training and development needs.

2.5 Responsibility for training and developing employees is clearly identified and understood throughout the organisation, starting at the top.

2.6 Objectives are set for training and development actions at the organisation, team and individual level.

3.1 All new employees are introduced effectively to the organisation and all employees new to a job are given the training and development they need to do that job.

3.2 Managers are effective in carrying out their responsibilities for training and developing employees.

3.3 Managers are actively involved in supporting employees to meet their training and development needs.

3.6 Action takes place to meet the training and development needs of individuals, teams and the organisation.

8 Reviewing and Applying the Learning

This chapter looks at arguably the most challenging part of the Investors in People process – evaluation. In it, we contend that it is impossible for effective evaluation to take place without careful planning and the setting of clear objectives in advance of any training and development. We look at the different approaches and mechanisms used by a range of organisations to evaluate training and development, with special reference to Investors in People. Included are details of the manager's role in evaluation and the gathering of information to enable the organisation to ascertain the effectiveness of the training and development.

What is evaluation?

The *Oxford English Dictionary* defines to evaluate as: 'to find out or state the value of, to assess'. This definition is most appropriate when looking at evaluating training and development, especially in relation to Investors in People.

To evaluate the effectiveness of the training and development the following questions need to be addressed:

- Did the training and development activity meet its objectives?
- Is the person (or team or organisation) now able to do what you wanted them to be able to do?
- What difference has it made to performance?
- What has been the benefit(s) of the training and development?

These questions relate, in sequence, to the Investors in People indicators 4.1 to 4.4.

After answering each question you could ask the question, 'So what?' For example:

The training and development activity met its objectives of helping trainees to learn a range of new skills... *So what?*
The people are now able to do more than one job... *So what?*
People are more flexible and instead of sitting around waiting for work to come in, can help colleagues to do other jobs... *So what?*
The organisation (or team) benefits because work is completed more quickly, temporary staff are not needed to cover for absence, holidays etc, and therefore there is a clear cash saving.

Clearly the above process starts with a comparison between what was planned and what was achieved. Without objectives to compare achievements against, evaluation becomes at best subjective and often a rationalisation.

A close examination of the above questions will reveal they are a mirror image of those posed in Chapter 5 where we looked at *planning* for evaluation.

Another, complementary, way for managers to look at evaluation is to ask the following questions:

Did the person enjoy the event?
Did they learn anything?
Did they transfer the learning to the workplace?
Did the business benefit?

Frequently the only questions asked are the first two. There is also a danger that they are not necessarily related to the reason the person attended the event in the first place and therefore may again lead to subjective evaluation or rationalisation. However, not all the questions can be answered immediately. Evaluation therefore must be carried out in at least two stages: immediately after the event and some time later. Combining the first set of questions with the last set can lead to effective evaluation.

Before looking at methods it is worth remembering that the Investors in People indicators require evaluation to be carried out at three levels: organisational, team and individual. In very small organisations it may be difficult to separate the team and organisational levels.

So how do you do it?

At the end of the event

The first opportunity for evaluation is at the end of the event, ideally before leaving, and this process is therefore managed by the trainer or facilitator of the event. Most facilitators, whether they are in-house or external, have some kind of evaluation such as course critiques or reaction sheets, more commonly referred to as 'happy sheets'. They are a type of evaluation and if constructed carefully can give an immediate reaction as to whether the participant *thinks* the objectives have been met.

It is also possible to encourage people to review the event by including questions about what they have learnt, as illustrated in the example of a course critique included in Figure 8.1. Incidentally, 'happy sheets' can also be used to evaluate the various services that go into supporting an activity, such as catering and administration, and therefore can provide managers with additional useful information to refine further the training and development process.

Going through the above process can, therefore, contribute to evaluation evidence mainly at organisational level but may contribute at individual and team level too.

Post-event debriefs – immediately after

It is almost impossible for some kind of debrief not to take place. It is rare for a person to return from an event without someone (ideally the line manager) asking the questions, 'How did it go?', 'Was it helpful?', or perhaps, 'Did you enjoy it?' To make this more meaningful as an exercise in evaluation questions such as the following need to be asked:

'Was the event successful in meeting the objectives we agreed before the event?'
'How will you use the skills or apply the knowledge that you gained?'
'Do you now *think* you can do what we hoped you would be able to do, which we discussed before you went on the event?'
'When should we review how you are *using* the skills and knowledge?'

Part B of the evaluation form shown in Appendix 3 could be used at this stage in the evaluation process.

EVALUATION OF INVESTORS IN PEOPLE WORKSHOP

Line Manager's Role

Date:

Please indicate how satisfied you were against each question by ticking:

1 Very satisfied   2 Satisfied   3 Unsatisfied   4 Very unsatisfied

1. How successful was the workshop in meeting its aim and objectives?

	1	2	3	4
Aim	☐	☐	☐	☐
Objective (a)	☐	☐	☐	☐
Objective (b)	☐	☐	☐	☐
Objective (c)	☐	☐	☐	☐
Objective (d)	☐	☐	☐	☐
Objective (e)	☐	☐	☐	☐

Comments

2. How helpful was the workshop in meeting your objectives?

1	2	3	4
☐	☐	☐	☐

Was the length of the workshop: Too long ☐   About right ☐   Too short ☐

Comments

3. Can you make any suggestions to improve the workshop?

4. What were the three most important points you learnt during the workshop?

5. Are there any other Investors in People topics you would like to see addressed in future workshops?

Please indicate how you felt about:	1	2	3	4
Facilitator's presentation	☐	☐	☐	☐
Quality of handouts	☐	☐	☐	☐

Thank you.

Figure 8.1 *Example of a course critique or reaction sheet*

Post-event debriefs – after a while

It is amazing that many organisations and their managers miss this stage in evaluation. When asked how their manager knows whether the skills learnt on the training or developmental event are being used, many people simply don't know. Many managers simply *assume* that the skills will be used; others see that they are being used but don't acknowledge it with their people. In one case the manager, a Head of Department in a school, did it secretly by watching the teacher's performance through a crack in the door! How long after an event it is worth reviewing the application of skills and/or knowledge depends on the complexity of the training and development.

If a group of people attended an event, a post-event debriefing may contribute to evaluation at the team level as well as individual level.

The third part of the proforma shown in Appendix 3 could be used for this stage in the evaluation process.

Via the appraisal or training needs review process

As discussed in Chapter 5, to become an Investor in People an organisation needs a process to identify training and development needs. This process, whether it is an appraisal process or something else, should offer an opportunity for evaluation. Training and development objectives will have been agreed at the previous review; they should be discussed, along with how the activity has impacted on performance, before agreeing new objectives.

This is also the start of gathering information about the benefits of training and development.

Learning logs

Some organisations have encouraged individuals to keep learning logs. Although they may be seen as a bureaucratic chore, they can be very useful in a number of ways.

They come in various forms and often link to personal/individual development plans. Some individuals may keep them as a record which will contribute to their Continuous Professional Development (CPD), which many professional bodies require their members to demonstrate.

Learning logs are useful in that they enable the individual to review what has been learnt from training and/or developmental actions in a systematic way. Quite often, people (and we include ourselves here) return from training or developmental activities full of good intentions of reviewing the notes and handouts that have been given and of implementing some of the ideas that were suggested or thoughts that were triggered by the event. The good intentions often disappear under the volume of work that meets you on your return. The discipline of having a structured method of reviewing what was learnt and entering it in a learning log is a useful one to develop.

Unless there is a CPD requirement, keeping learning logs needs a discipline that is largely self-imposed. Those organisations that tried to introduce learning logs as a policy often found that a large number of people did not complete them because they can be time-consuming, especially if not done on a regular basis. It is therefore better for organisations, through managers, to sell the concept and the benefits rather than try to impose it.

Where learning logs are kept, they can contribute, at the individual level, to evaluation of what was learnt and how it has been applied.

Achievement of qualifications, including NVQs

This is probably the most straightforward form of evaluation. When the outcome of training and development is the achievement of a qualification, this indicates that the objectives of the activity have been met and therefore contributes to the evaluation of the effectiveness of the training.

Assessment of competence against National Standards through the NVQ process is another form of evaluation. However, it is also important, when using NVQ assessments to illustrate evaluation, to be able to demonstrate what has been *learnt* and how it has affected performance. In some cases the achievement of an NVQ may be merely confirming what the person has been able to do for some time and little learning may have taken place. While the achievement of the NVQ may have a motivational payback, especially if that person has never before had a piece of paper that says they are competent, the impact on performance may be marginal.

Sharing or cascading learning

In order to manage training budgets effectively, instead of sending a number of people on training events many organisations ask those who do attend to present a summary of the event to colleagues. There are a number of disadvantages to this method of training, especially if the 'presenter' is not trained in presentational skills. We have, however, seen this approach used effectively and it can offer managers the chance to monitor what *has* been learned and can therefore contribute to the evaluation of training and development.

Evaluation and project management

A large number of organisations will at some stage involve their staff in project work. For some, such as construction and civil engineering companies, property consultants, etc, their whole business is made up of projects. For example, at Ealing, Hammersmith and Hounslow Health Authority, a large part of their 'business' is concerned with projects to improve the health of the people in their area. Another example is the Health and Safety Laboratory at Sheffield, part of the Health and Safety Executive. A large amount of their work is project-based, either investigating the causes of accidents at work or carrying out research on behalf of clients who wish to prevent the accidents in the first place.

To have a successful project there must be a project plan and part of that plan is likely to involve initial research at the very least. Experts may well be brought in to offer advice and guidance, but throughout the project there will be a great deal of *learning* which may or may not be caught in the end-of-project report. It is not always easy to capture this type of learning but if it is planned into the project at an early stage it can contribute to effective evaluation.

Evaluation and continuous improvement

In a similar way, learning through continuous improvement projects or groups may contribute to evaluation. Again, it may not always have been planned to identify such learning but with a little thought at the planning stage it should be possible to capture sufficient information about increases in knowledge and/or skills. Sometimes it is difficult to separate the 'learning' from other outcomes, especially if the improvement focused on improved systems or processes, in which case some aspects of learning will merely be implied.

Avoiding the paperchase

There is often a concern regarding the potential bureaucracy of Investors in People and, without care, evaluation in particular can become very bureaucratic. It is therefore important to examine the processes that already exist and see if they can be used to help with evaluation.

A lot of the most essential processes mentioned above have already been mentioned earlier in this book and, for those organisations working towards Investors in People, will probably already exist or will have been introduced to satisfy earlier criteria. With just a little tweaking they can be used for evaluative purposes. We are always loath to add more paperwork, but the process of debriefing is easy to forget if it is not part of the culture or managers are not naturally people managers. It is therefore advisable, especially in the early stages, to have a paper system (such as the form in Appendix 3) which prompts managers to carry out these debriefs. It also enables organisations to 'audit' the post-training activity until debriefing becomes embedded in and therefore part of the culture, when the paperwork could become redundant.

Evaluating development

In Chapter 6 we examined methods of development. Because development may be less tangible than training, evaluation is not always that easy, as the following illustration shows. During the course of an Investors in People assessment, one of us interviewed a person who, he had been informed, had been 'developed'. When the person was asked how she had learnt the job she was doing she said she had 'picked it up'. It was only after a great deal of probing that the interviewee remembered that she had 'picked it up' through a well-structured development programme with a number of distinct activities that formed the programme. This therefore prompts the question, 'How do you evaluate development?'

There could be a temptation to evaluate every single developmental activity (although it is evident that many organisations are not so tempted!) In Chapter 6 we floated the idea of clustering developmental activities into 'programmes' or developmental projects. Although the three-stage form in Appendix 3 could be used as a pre-programme briefing, it would be simpler to use the appraisal or review process as the vehicle for setting aims and objectives and reviewing them. For those organisations which encourage the use of personal development plans, they would be the vehicle for evaluating effectiveness.

Agreeing and recording aims and objectives and evaluating the 'development programme' is therefore the simple and unbureaucratic method of evaluating 'development'. It may also avoid people who have been developed saying that they merely 'picked it up'.

Evaluating the impact of training and development

Many organisations find this is difficult to do. The first question to ask is, 'Did the training and/or development have the planned effect?' This implies of course that there was a *planned*, desired effect. As we have often reiterated, effective evaluation does not mean scratching heads and trying to work out what effect the training contribution has had after the event. Effective evaluation is checking actual outcomes against planned outcomes. There will of course be 'by-products', those unintended outcomes (hopefully beneficial!) and these should also be acknowledged, but the simplest approach to evaluation is based on having 'SMART' objectives at the planning stage (see Chapter 5).

This is as relevant at the organisational level as it is at the team and individual level. It is not as simple at the organisational level, especially in larger organisations. It often means having some system for collating information gathered at team and individual levels. This may imply a layer of bureaucracy but it does not need to. In the early chapters of this book we described how organisations used a meetings structure to inform employees. The same structure can be used to pass information back up to the top about the effectiveness and benefits of training and development.

Some organisations use written processes to gather such information, with formal procedures or written reviews of training and development presented to senior management meetings. Whatever method is chosen it is important that it works; if it doesn't – change it.

This then links to the evaluation of systems. As Investors in People is aligned to Total Quality and therefore continuous improvement, it is important that the effectiveness of the training and development systems and processes is reviewed too. This is especially important when they are new.

Did we get value for money?

In Chapter 3 the need to know the costs and benefits of training is seen as part of the role of senior managers. The question of getting value for money is often a difficult one for many senior managers to answer. Perhaps the question should be reworded – 'Did you get the *planned* value for money?

Throughout this book we have referred to the need to link training and development to the needs of the organisation and the need to set SMART objectives. Part of this SMARTness should really include the anticipated return on the investment of time and money in delivering the training and development.

It really comes back to what the business objective was. For example, was the training and development and subsequent increased application of skills and/or knowledge supposed to lead to an increase in production? To save time? To improve service in order to get repeat business?

All of these can be measured and given an anticipated monetary value, as can the cost of the training and development in terms of time and/or money spent. After a period of time following the training, a comparison of the cost of the training against the *actual* improvements in terms of increased production, time saved etc, can give you a simple cost-benefit analysis which shows whether value for money was achieved.

Many readers will now be saying that it's not as simple as that! It's not possible to measure the impact of some training in those terms. They will probably cite management training as an example. But why are managers trained and/or developed? To be less efficient? If they are more efficient will they not:

- Carry out their job in less time?
- Or juggle more balls at the same time?
- Or manage their time more efficiently?
- Or get more efficiency from their people?

Again, all these things could be measured in some way and a value placed on the improvements. This of course could become quite complex and it is at this point that a judgement has to be made whether value for money is being achieved from carrying out the cost-benefit analysis itself. We do believe if the measures are kept fairly simple, while the cost-benefit analysis may not satisfy the purists, it would give a rough idea of value for money. Without trying to establish value for money how do you know the money is not being wasted?

If all else fails ask yourself the simple question: 'If this was my money, would I still spend it on the training and development?' If the answer is yes, then ask yourself, why? The answer to the second question will go some way to proving whether you are getting value for money. A handy checklist, usable at the individual, team and organisational level, is shown in Figure 8.2.

Summary

This chapter has examined the evaluation of training in the context of Investors in People. It has examined a variety of methods and useful, but simple, approaches. It has described the roles that managers at all levels should have in the evaluation process and how they can contribute to gathering information on behalf of the organisation as whole, including whether value for money is being achieved.

Self-Audit

☐ *What are you trying to do?*
☐ *Why are you trying to do it?*
☐ *How are you trying to do it?*
☐ *Why are you doing it that way?*
☐ *Is it the best way of doing it?*
☐ *Is it effective?*
☐ *How do you check its effectiveness?*
☐ *What do you do as a result of the check?*

(New Zealand Universities Academic Audit Unit, 1995)

Figure 8.2 *An evaluation checklist*

What do managers need to do?

- Immediately after returning from an event, check what was learnt and whether the participant *thinks* the objectives agreed before the event were met.
- After an appropriate time discuss with the participant whether the skills and knowledge are being used and whether they are able to achieve what was expected prior to the event taking place.
- During appraisals or reviews, check that previously set *learning* objectives have been met
- Try to capture information about what has been learnt through project work or continuous improvement activity.
- Keep a simple record of benefits to the person, team or organisation so that it can be passed on to senior managers or whoever is responsible for collating such information at the organisational level.

Reference

New Zealand Universities Academic Audit Unit (1995) *Audit Manual: Handbook for institutions and members of audit panels.*

THE RELEVANT INVESTORS IN PEOPLE INDICATORS

2.1 A written but flexible plan sets out the organisation's goals and targets.

2.2 A written plan identifies the organisation's training and development needs, and specifies what action will be taken to meet these needs.

2.3 Training and development needs are regularly reviewed against goals and targets at the organisation, team and individual level.

2.6 Objectives are set for training and development actions at the organisation, team and individual level.

2.7 Where appropriate, training and development needs are linked to external standards such as National Vocational Qualifications (NVQs) or Scottish Vocational Qualifications (SVQs) and units.

3.2 Managers are effective in carrying out their responsibilities for training and developing employees.

3.3 Managers are actively involved in supporting employees to meet their training and development needs.

4.1 The organisation evaluates the impact of training and development actions on knowledge, skills and attitude.

4.2 The organisation evaluates the impact of training and development actions on performance.

4.3 The organisation evaluates the contribution of training and development to the achievement of its goals and targets.

4.4 Top management understands the broad costs and benefits of training and developing employees.

4.5 Action takes place to implement improvements to training and development identified as a result of evaluation.

Part 3 Following Recognition

9 The Manager's Role in Retaining Investors in People Status

With some 5,200 organisations recognised, some of whom will be reassessed for the second time during 1997, it is necessary to explore the manager's role in retaining the recognition as an Investor in People.

This chapter looks at some of the pitfalls, 'traps' and obstacles we have met while working with organisations which are approaching reassessment, and offers some thoughts as to how managers can help avoid or overcome them.

Post-recognition euphoria

Clearly, when an organisation is recognised as an Investor in People it is time for celebration. The level of euphoria will be related to the amount of effort put into preparing the organisation for assessment. We have often referred to recognition as being a 'milestone on a journey'. For organisations which have used the Investors in People principles for a long time, the effort may well not have been as great as for those which have introduced them more recently.

It is those organisations for which the first major milestone *is* recognition that are the most vulnerable to letting systems slip into disuse. In these organisations people will have worked hard to achieve the standard. There will be a 'plateau' period directly after recognition. It is possible that this period may become extended. This should not happen where systems are embedded, but it does.

Why do systems fall into disuse?

The reasons for this are many and varied. Sometimes, quite simply, systems are not as embedded as they should be, or as senior staff think they are. The guidance from Investors in People UK states that assessors should ensure that systems are embedded, especially new ones. This generally means that they have been used twice and reviewed and improved. When interviewing, assessors will try to judge whether the people agree that systems have become embedded. They will also wish to ascertain if the systems would actually be missed if for any reason they fell into disuse.

As we have suggested throughout this book, systems rely on managers and their commitment to making them work. Clearly the responsibility to *continue* the use of the systems also falls back on to managers. Quite often, when systems have fallen into disuse, it is because they are too complex and/or time-consuming. Managers have found them to be a chore – a bolt-on activity, not part of 'normal' work – and have therefore stopped using them. Unless there are procedures in place to pick this up it may not be noticed until reassessment approaches.

Gaining recognition through linking Investors in People to a major in-house programme

Many organisations have coupled major initiatives with their approach to Investors in People, such as a customer care programme. It makes a lot of sense and it may well make it easier to demonstrate improvements through training and development, especially if the organisation was starting from a low baseline. However, success with these programmes may also lead to a false sense of security and things may again plateau. Even if the programme continues it is unlikely that previously impressive results will keep appearing. It is therefore essential for managers to be aware of this potentiality and to look for ways of seeking further improvements. At the same time, they should make people aware that improvements may not be on the same *scale* as before, but are just as important.

Continuous improvement

We have found that organisations which have approached Investors in People from a Total Quality or continuous improvement angle are, in the main, more aware of the pitfalls. They are also less likely to allow systems to slip. The ethos of continual review and looking for a better way of doing things means that complex systems would be reviewed and simplified. They will be continuously keeping abreast of the latest trends and ideas and assessing their relevance to their own organisations.

They will not assume anything, as they are also likely to have quality monitoring and evaluation procedures that show if and when systems are falling into disuse. Action would then be taken to investigate why this was happening or perhaps just to remind people to take appropriate action. Taking this type of action will avoid the last-minute (or months') panic when it is realised that the date for reassessment is fast approaching.

IBM Education and Training realised that they could not sit back following recognition. They intended to take a number of actions:

1. Continue to canvas employee opinion by repeating their diagnostic survey annually.
2. Involve their managers through a process of self-assessment against the Investors in People indicators.
3. Through the above process they intend risk-banding any activity, or lack of it, in line with their quality policy. Following the risk-banding, action would take place as follows:
   Red: High risk   Requires urgent action
   Amber: Low risk   Requires action
   Green: No risk   Some minor action may be required.
4. Keeping a training and development scorecard. This involved recording factual information about the number of people trained and developed each month, comparing it with previous years, and recording student satisfaction.
5. They are also planning to introduce the management NVQs.

It is interesting to compare what has been written in this book with what Deming, one of the Total Quality gurus, called his '14 points'; these are reproduced below:

1. Create constancy of purpose for the improvement of product and service.

2. Adopt the new philosophy for the new economic age with management learning what their responsibilities are, and by assuming leadership.
3. Cease dependence on mass inspection to achieve quality by building quality into the product.
4. End the practice of awarding business on price tag alone.
5. Improve constantly and forever the system of production and service.
6. Institute training and retraining.
7. Institute leadership with the aim of supervising people to help them do a better job.
8. Drive out fear so that everyone can work effectively together for the organisation.
9. Break down barriers between departments..
10. Eliminate slogans, exhortations and targets for the workforce.
11. Eliminate numerical quotas.
12. Remove barriers to pride of workmanship.
13. Institute a vigorous programme of education and a self-improvement programme.
14. Put everyone in the company to work to accomplish the transformation.

While not all are directly related to the Investors in People issues we have referred to throughout this book, there are certainly a number of overlaps, especially those concerned with continuous improvement through management, leadership, communication and of course training and development. Training and development and *learning* are at the heart of continuous improvement and therefore at the heart of Total Quality.

Evaluating learning through continuous improvement

As organisations move away from formal training and into learning through continuous improvement, the *learning* becomes less tangible. It therefore becomes more difficult to evaluate the impact of the learning as distinct from the *improvement* which may often be to do with systems and processes. Some may question whether there is a need to distinguish the learning in this way: to retain Investors in People status it may be necessary in the absence of more traditional and tangible training activity. In Chapter 8 we referred to learning logs and how we found that some people keep them to record what they have learnt and how the learning may be applied. Encouraging people to do this could be a way of satisfying an assessor. It will also fulfil CPD requirements for those who need to.

Senior managers and *continued* commitment

The first thing for senior managers to remember to recognise is that retaining Investors in People status needs effort too. The good practice concerning the *demonstration* of their commitment mentioned in Chapter 3 should be continued, but other senior manager actions are also required. If little or nothing more is done by senior managers it will reinforce in the minds of the cynics that they were only committed to getting the badge and not to the principles and philosophy of Investors in People.

What do senior managers need to do?

The continued use of systems and processes should identify the successes brought about through training and development. It should become part of the culture of the organisation that senior managers, especially, publicly acknowledge the part that training and development have played in business success and that they will therefore *continue* to be committed to them.

They should encourage the philosophy of continuous improvement being extended to improving the training and development itself and the processes and systems that underpin it. Standing still is not good enough.

Summary

This chapter has examined the manager's role in retaining Investors in People status and related it to the concept of Total Quality. It has pointed out a number of the pitfalls and made suggestions as to how to avoid them. Finally, it has reminded senior managers of the need to *continue* to be committed to training and developing their people and how this can be demonstrated.

Reference

Walton, M (1989) *The Deming Management Method*, London: Mercury.

THE RELEVANT INVESTORS IN PEOPLE INDICATORS

1.1 The commitment from top management to train and develop employees is communicated effectively throughout the organisation.

1.2 Employees at all levels are aware of the broad aims or vision of the organisation.

1.3 The employer has considered what employees at all levels will contribute to the success of the organisation, and has communicated this effectively to them.

2.3 Training and development needs are regularly reviewed against goals and targets at the organisation, team and individual level.

2.4 A written plan identifies the resources that will be used to meet training and development needs.

3.3 Managers are actively involved in supporting employees to meet their training and development needs.

3.6 Action takes place to meet the training and development needs of individuals, teams and the organisation.

4.3 The organisation evaluates the contribution of training and development to the achievement of its goals and targets.

4.4 Top management understands the broad costs and benefits of training and developing employees.

4.5 Action takes place to implement improvements to training and development identified as a result of evaluation.

4.6 Top management's continuing commitment to training and developing employees is demonstrated to all employees.

Appendix 1
The National Standard
for Effective Investment
in People and Related
Management Actions

INDICATOR	MANAGEMENT ACTIONS
Principle 1: Commitment *An Investor in People makes a commitment from the top to develop all employees to achieve its business objectives.*	
1.1 The commitment from top management to train and develop employees is communicated effectively throughout the organisation.	Senior management, as well as stating 'people are our greatest asset' or similar, should demonstrate their commitment through actions. Showing interest, walking the floor, etc are needed on a regular basis to convince employees of their commitment.
	Line managers should support senior manager commitment by reinforcing at appropriate times.
1.2 Employees at all levels are aware of the broad aims or vision of the organisation.	Senior management should have a clear vision of where the organisation is going and communicate it to all employees through periodic meetings, newsletters, etc.
	Line managers/supervisors should reinforce regularly and ensure that the vision is understood by all staff.
1.3 The organisation has considered what employees at all levels will contribute to the success of the organisation, and has communicated this effectively to them.	Line managers should ensure that employees know where they 'fit in' and feel they do contribute, and that they are clear how they contribute. This should be reinforced at every opportunity, through meetings, personal reviews etc.
1.4 Where representative structures exist, communication takes place between management and representatives on the vision of where the organisation is going and the contribution that employees (and their representatives) will make to its success.	If trade unions are recognised by the organisation, senior managers should communicate their intentions to them.

INDICATOR	MANAGEMENT ACTIONS
Principle 2: Planning. *An Investor in People regularly reviews the needs and plans the training and development of all employees.* 2.1 A written but flexible plan sets out the organisation's goals and targets.	Senior managers ideally need to set the broad objectives and targets for the organisation and present them to line managers/supervisors for their input. Line managers/supervisors should then, as far as practicable, consult and involve employees when their operational plans are being compiled. They should create an atmosphere that encourages employees to contribute ideas. Whether involved in the process or not, all employees should be made aware of the goals and targets.
2.2 A written plan identifies the organisation's training and development needs, and specifies what action will be taken to meet these needs.	Senior managers should identify what they believe to be the broad training and development needs required to achieve the organisational objectives and communicate them to line managers/supervisors. Line managers/supervisors need to ensure that all employees understand these broad development needs as these, and the organisational objectives, set a context for all training and development.
2.3 Training and development needs are regularly reviewed against goals and targets at the organisation, team and individual level.	Senior managers should periodically review the organisation's progress towards meeting the broad development needs. If changes in organisational goals occur, they should review the training and development implications. Line managers should carry out regular discussions with their staff to identify and agree training and development needs. This may be through appraisal if such a process exists.
2.4 A written plan identifies the resources that will be used to meet training and development needs.	Senior managers should ensure sufficient resource is available – time, money, people, facilities, etc to meet those broad needs and any justifiable training and development areas identified through the reviews. Line managers should ensure staff understand that there are resources and, if necessary, that they are limited.
2.5 Responsibility for training and developing employees is clearly identified and understood throughout the organisation, starting at the top.	Senior managers should ensure that it is clear at *all* levels in the organisation who is responsible for training and developing people. These responsibilities should be clearly identified. Where line managers' job descriptions/role specifications exist, they should include reference to their responsibilities for developing people.
2.6 Objectives are set for training and development actions at the organisation, team and individual level.	Senior managers should set the organisational objectives for training and development, ie, the difference they expect the training and development to make at an organisational level. Before employees undertake any training or development line managers/supervisors should agree with them what is expected from the training or development actions – what people (either individually or in groups) are expected to learn. They should also clarify and agree how the learning will be applied, ie, what they will be able to do after the activity that they were unable to do before.
2.7 Where appropriate, training and development needs are linked to external standards, such as National Vocational Qualifications (NVQs) or Scottish Vocational Qualifications (SVQs) and units.	Senior managers should develop a policy on the use of external qualifications and ensure that line managers are aware so that they can encourage their use as appropriate.

INDICATOR	MANAGEMENT ACTIONS
Principle 3: Action. *An Investor in People takes action to train and develop individuals on recruitment and throughout their employment.*	Senior managers should ensure that there is a clear policy on induction especially at organisational level and make sure line managers carry out their responsibilities at department/section level.
3.1 All new employees are introduced effectively to the organisation and all employees new to a job are given the training and development they need to do that job.	Line managers/supervisors should ensure that *all* new staff are properly inducted to the organisation, the job and the people with whom they will be working. When people change jobs line managers should ensure that any training and development needs are identified and that they are inducted into their new role.
3.2 Managers are effective in carrying out their responsibilities for training and developing employees.	Senior managers should be clear how they define what managers should do to be effective in carrying out the responsibilities identified in indicator 2.5. This means that *all* line managers are trained and developed to enable them to carry out their role. This also links to indicator 2.3 – the regular review for line managers should review people management skills. The use of NVQs and Management Standards should be considered.
3.3 Managers are actively involved in supporting employees to meet their training and development needs.	*All* line managers/supervisors should create an atmosphere that encourages their staff to seek continuous development and improvement. Active support links to effectiveness and includes appraising, coaching, etc to develop people. This indicator is about *commitment* to training and development at the line manager level (similar to 1.1).
3.4 All employees are made aware of the training and development opportunities open to them.	The organisation, through line managers/supervisors, should ensure that all staff are made aware of training and development opportunities.
3.5 All employees are encouraged to help identify and meet their job-related training and development needs.	Line managers/supervisors, as part of their coaching/support role, should encourage their people to take responsibility for their own development – part of active support in indicator 3.3.
3.6 Action takes place to meet the training and development needs of individuals, teams, and the organisation.	When training and development needs have been identified (in 1.4), line managers/supervisors should ensure that the action to meet them takes place. When training and development needs have been identified by individuals or by groups (as in 2.3/3.5) line managers/supervisors should ensure that the action to meet them takes place.

INDICATOR	MANAGEMENT ACTIONS
Principle 4: Evaluation. *An Investor in People evaluates the investment in training and development to assess achievement and improve future effectiveness.* 4.1 The organisation evaluates the impact of training and development actions on knowledge, skills and attitude.	This involves all managers. When people return from training and development activities they should ask whether staff now feel they have the skills and/or knowledge to enable them to do what was agreed in indicator 2.6 (or indicator 2.3). Achievement of qualifications may also demonstrate effectiveness. It may also involve training specialists evaluating their actions through course critiques.
4.2 The organisation evaluates the impact of training and development actions on performance.	This indicator involves line managers/supervisors in observing and monitoring the work of their staff following the training and development activity to ensure that they are using the new skills and knowledge and it is having the desired effect on performance. If not, then further action may be needed.
4.3 The organisation evaluates the contribution of training and development to the achievement of its goals and targets.	This is about evaluating the impact of the organisation's training and development actions on the business *as a whole*. Senior managers should ensure that the effectiveness of the training and development activities taken to meet the broad goals in 2.2 is evaluated and the impact on the business goals in 2.1 assessed – ie, are people in the organisation using the new skills or applying the newly acquired knowledge? What difference has it made? Have the original business objectives been achieved? Information may be gathered in a variety of ways – training and development actions that have included everyone in the organisation will probably be gathered centrally; in other cases, line mangers will probably need to supply information on local activities so that it can be collated centrally.
4.4 Top management understands the broad costs and benefits of training and developing employees.	This will mainly concern senior managers, but the information may be supplied by line managers/supervisors. Senior managers should be aware of the full cost, ie opportunity costs, cost of staff cover, as well as the actual cost of the training. They should be quite clear about the benefits, ie the impact on the business as a whole. Is it clear that training and development contributed to the achievement of the business objectives? Senior managers should be able to articulate this information and make the linkages. Training and development should not be an act of faith.
4.5 Action takes place to implement improvements to training and development identified as a result of evaluation.	Where evaluation identifies the need, senior managers, through their line managers and, perhaps, their training and development specialists, introduce changes to training and development activities or processes. This should be an ongoing task for managers as part of a continuous improvement culture.
4.6 Top management's continuing commitment to training and developing employees is demonstrated to all employees.	Senior managers should demonstrate through communications and actions that the commitment in 1.1 is continuous. They should encourage further development through celebrating the benefits of successful training and development activities, achievement of qualifications, etc. This should include benefits to individuals as well as at team and organisational levels. Line managers should reinforce this commitment to ensure their staff believe it.

Appendix 2
Sources of Help

This is a 'Who's who' of the various sources of help available to assist organisations through the process.

As addresses and telephone numbers can soon become out of date, it does not give full details of all the sources. It does not attempt to list all sources but merely points to the key players who in turn may have their own sources to which they redirect anyone who wants to know more.

Investors in People UK

Investors in People UK was established in July 1993 as a private company limited by guarantee. It opened for business on 1 October 1993. It has a board chaired by Sir Brian Wolfson and an executive arm.

Chief Executive	Mary Chapman
Address:	7/10 Chandos Street, London W1M 9DE
Tel:	0171 467 1900

The role of Investors in People UK is:

– to guard, lead and direct the Investors in People Standard;
– define the assessment process in outline;
– national promotion and support;
– national quality assurance;
– assessment and recognition of national organisations, TECs/LECs and Industry Training Organisations.

Investors in People UK works in close consultation with all its partners.

Training and Enterprise Councils (TECs)

TECs were set up by the government in the late 1980s to deliver products and services such as Youth and Adult Training, establish education partnerships and generally support Enterprise Start-up in specific geographical areas throughout England and Wales.

TECs are independent companies limited by guarantee and driven strategically by a Board of Directors drawn in the main from key people in local business communities but also from the public and voluntary sector. The Board's role is to ensure that the portfolio of services offered meets the local needs.

There are 81 TECs covering all of England and Wales. They work in partnership with other key local organisations, working towards the economic regeneration of their areas.

They also have the task of encouraging employers to train and develop their existing workforce in order to develop the skill base on which the future prosperity of the country will depend, which is where Investors in People fits in.

TECs are responsible for the local delivery of Investors in People. This means they are responsible for marketing and promotion, advice and guidance, assessment and recognition. They deliver this in a variety of ways. All TECs receive funding from central government, mainly from the Department for Education and Employment, to help support enterprise activities. This budget has gradually been reduced and therefore financial support for Investors in People from TECs is limited and varies from one TEC to another.

The number of staff working on Investors in People also varies from TEC to TEC, with most using outside help to deliver the initiative. Later in this appendix the role of this outside help, mainly in the form of consultants, is described.

An increasing number of TECs are offering workshops or seminars which are geared to helping organisations through the process. Some TECs will offer these free and others will make a nominal charge. If nothing else, these workshops will introduce you to other organisations that are going through the process, and they will often be very willing to share ideas, problems, etc.

The telephone numbers and addresses of TECs can be found in local telephone directories.

Scotland – Local Enterprise Companies (LECs)

The position in Scotland is different. LECs were set up at about the same time as TECs but they have a wider remit as they not only took over the delivery of products and services such as Youth and Adult Training but also embraced the role of the Scottish Development Agency and the Highlands and Islands Development Agency.

LECs too are private companies limited by guarantee who are contracted to either Scottish Enterprise or Highlands and Islands Enterprise. There are 22 LECs, although some counts might show 23 as one straddles the border between Scottish Enterprise and Highlands and Islands Enterprise and is often counted twice.

Assessment and recognition is carried out by Investors in People Scotland so the role of the LECs is to carry out the same work as TECs minus assessment and recognition. They too use outsiders to deliver various stages of Investors in People.

The telephone numbers and addresses of LECs can be found in local telephone directories.

Northern Ireland – Training and Employment Agency (T&EA)

The T&EA was established as an agency of the Northern Ireland Civil Service in 1990. It carries out a role similar to that of the Employment Agency in mainland Britain, ie a training and job-broking service.

One of its divisions has a particular remit to support business and it is within this remit that Investors in People sits.

The Agency has broadly the same role as the TECs in delivering Investors in People. However, the financial support offered by the Agency is through its Company Development Programme and the consultants who deliver it.

Investors In People Scotland

Investors in People Scotland is also a company limited by guarantee. It was originally set up to carry out assessments on behalf of the Scottish LECs.

All the work prior to assessment is carried out by the LECs.

Address: 13 Abercromby Place, Edinburgh EH3 6LB
Tel: 0131 557 0333

Management Charter Initiative (MCI)

For information on the Management Standards or the report, *Investors in People and the Management Standards*, contact MCI.

Address: Russell Square House, 10–12 Russell Square,
          London WC1B 5BZ
Tel: 0171 872 9000

Industry Training Organisations (ITOs)

ITOs act as the principal focal point for training matters in their particular sector of industry. They are employer led and funded bodies and often linked to existing employer associations. Their tasks are to see that the skills needs of their sector are being met and that appropriate standards are established and maintained for key occupations in their sector. There are currently about 120 ITOs – one for most industrial sectors of the country.

A number of ITOs may be able to offer support through the Investors in People process. There is a National Council of ITOs (NCITO) that can supply more information.

Address: 10 Amos Road, Unit 10 Meadow Court,
          Sheffield S9 1BX
Tel: 0114 261 9926

The future of ITOs has been reviewed and during late 1997 their responsibilities are to be transferred to newly formed National Training Organisations, which are likely to have an expanded role. Further information will be available from NCITO.

National Council for Vocational Qualifications (NCVQ)

This organisation is responsible for overseeing the development and promotion of National Vocational Qualifications.

Address: 222 Euston Road, London NW1 2BZ
Tel: 0171 387 9898

From late 1997 this organisation's work will be the responsibility of the Qualifications and National Curriculum Authority.

The Universities' and Colleges' Staff Development Agency (UCoSDA)

UCoSDA was created in 1989. It is one of the agencies of the Committee of Vice Chancellors and Principals.

UCoSDA seeks to provide advice, support and resources to its member universities and colleges in the planning, organisation, provision and evaluation of continuing professional/vocational development for all personnel in the higher education sector.

It currently employs two approved Investors in People assessors, including one of the authors of this book. The UCoSDA philosophy captures some of the central themes of this book and is summarised as follows:

> Investment in the personal, professional and vocational development of all staff employed by universities and colleges is fundamental
> (a) to the successful achievement of organisational goals and
> (b) to the motivation and continuing capacity of individual staff members to support that achievement.

UCoSDA has produced a number of briefing papers and other publications on Investors in People and related issues.

Address: Ingram House, 65 Wilkinson Street, The University of
           Sheffield, Sheffield S10 2GJ
Tel: 0114 282 4211
Fax: 0114 272 8705

Consultants and consultancy organisations

Feelings about using consultants differ considerably from one organisation or person to another. This book does not intend to debate the merits or otherwise of using consultants; the arguments are well rehearsed elsewhere.

However, because the resources within TECs and LECs are limited most, if not all organisations, use outside help to deliver the various stages of Investors in People. Because TECs and LECs are so reliant on using consultants, Investors in People UK has developed criteria for establishing the ability of the consultants to deliver what is required.

If you feel a consultant is needed to help your organisation, the first stage is to be clear what it is you want the consultant to do. This may involve a discussion with someone from the Investors team at the local TEC or LEC.

Choosing and using consultants

The next stage is to ensure the consultant is qualified to do what you want them to deliver. This is probably easier said than done as there are so many consultants touting for work. Some simple questions to ask are:

- How many companies have you helped to achieve recognition?
- Which TECs/LECs are you working with?
- What training have you had in connection with Investors in People?
- Are you an accredited assessor? How many assessments have you carried out?
- What is your approach to helping organisations achieve Investors in People status? (Beware of those consultants who say they will get it for you and have a sure fire way of meeting a number of indicators! They may sell you a package that you don't want or need.)
- What sector expertise do you bring? (In some cases having sector expertise may save time with interpreting the Standard but it is not always essential.)

How consultants can help

Provided you get the right consultant they can help in a number of ways. First, they may have experience working with TECs/LECs and may help you secure some financial support. They should have experience of carrying out certain tasks and can therefore help you avoid reinventing wheels.

They *should* know what is expected of you by an assessor, but make sure that you are not merely introducing things for an assessor but are doing them for sound business reasons too. In most cases the needs of the assessor will coincide with your needs, but you need constantly to challenge the consultant (or TEC staff for that matter) if you feel you are being asked to do something from which you will gain no business benefits.

When consultants can help

Our previous book, *Investors in People Explained*, described the Investors in People process in three broad stages:

- diagnosis and action planning;
- advice and guidance with implementation of plans;
- assessment.

Diagnosis and action planning

To get an honest response from staff it is almost essential that an out-sider is used to help carry out this stage of the process. It is also the stage when you will be least able to interpret the responses against the indicators, so bringing in a consultant experienced in carrying out this exercise will save a lot of time.

The main health warning here concerns the writing of the action plan. Consultants should carry out the diagnosis and analysis against the indicators and present the issues to you. These issues should cover those indicators that appear to be satisfied and those that do not. Generally they can be grouped under a number of headings (see Taylor and Thackwray, 1996). It is the job of the people within the organisation to decide how they want to tackle these issues – a good consultant will stand back at this stage and allow you to do so. They may help you present the action plan, filling in stages that might have been overlooked or presenting it in a way that meets TEC requirements if funding is being sought.

We have seen too many action plans written by consultants that have not been implemented because they are not 'owned' by the organisation for which they were written.

Advice and guidance with implementation of plans

The action plan should include what external help you may need to help you through the process. We believe this should be kept to a minimum as most organisations, even small ones, should be able to devise and introduce most systems, processes and practices that they need to meet their business requirements and at the same time meet the requirements of the indicators.

There are of course a number of exceptions, such as introducing strategic planning for the first time, or introducing an appraisal process, but remember – this is *not* a requirement of the Standard.

Most organisations will need some kind of management develop-ment and may need support for managers at all levels; it could be helpful to have an outsider facilitate this.

Be careful about consultants who try to persuade you that you need large amounts of consultancy input to meet the Standard. Experience has shown that most organisations will need some 'hand-holding' through the process. This will involve attendance at meetings to discuss progress and to nudge the organisation along. When it comes to building a portfolio, outside help from someone who understands how to present your case to an assessor will be useful.

Some TECs/LECs will offer this service but with others you may need a consultant.

Assessment

This is one stage where you may have no option but to have a consultant in your organisation. The TEC, or other Assessment and Recognition Unit, decides who will carry out the assessment and their policy may be to use consultants for this role.

Any dissatisfaction with the assessor should be reported back to the TEC Investors Manager.

Other organisations

The help offered by peers who are going through the process was mentioned earlier, but what about those organisations who have already been recognised? The first organisations were inundated with callers who wanted to know how they did it; some of them may well have wondered why they got involved! However, now there are a lot more people to offer this kind of guidance.

Most TECs and LECs invite representatives from recognised organisations to speak at local events, so you may well find out about them then. If not, or if you need to identify a specific type of organisation, your TEC or LEC will be able to put you in touch with some one who can help.

Investors in People material, videos, etc

Finally, there are many materials available to help you work through the process. Most TECs have produced their own material, but there is also lots of national material produced by Investors in People UK.

There is also plenty of material in the form of articles in management and training magazines and books (this is one!) to help you understand what Investors in People is and how it can help you.

Reference

Taylor, P and Thackwray, R (1996) *Investors in People Explained*, 2nd edn, London: Kogan Page.

Appendix 3
Sample Evaluation Sheet

EVALUATION OF TRAINING AND DEVELOPMENT EFFECTIVENESS

Name: _____

Section/Department: _____

Part A. Prior to the training or development action

1. Proposed training/development activity _____

2. Details, eg, dates, locations, cost _____
_____

3. The business objective the proposed activity will help to achieve
_____

4. The skills and/or knowledge that will be learnt as a result of the activity
_____

5. How the new skills and/or knowledge will be applied after the activity
_____

6. Line manager's comments, ie, expectations in terms of targets or standards
_____
_____

Signatures _____ Participant _____ date

_____ Line manager _____ date

Part B. Immediately after the training and/or developmental activity

1. Did the participant attend _____ yes/no (if no give reason)

_____

_____

2. To what extent has this activity met the agreed training and/or development need?

Please circle   Not at all   1   2   3   4   Totally

Comments

_____

_____

3. How will the learning be applied?

_____

_____

4. What help/support is needed to put the learning into practice?

_____

_____

5. To what extent did the activity represent:

Value for money

Please circle   Not at all   1   2   3   4   Totally

An acceptable standard of delivery

Please circle   Not at all   1   2   3   4   Totally

Comments

_____

_____

6. Agreed date to review

Signatures _____   Participant _____ date

_____   Line manager _____ date

Part C. Review to monitor impact on performance

1. How has the learning been applied since the activity?

_____

_____

2. To what extent have the agreed objectives/targets or standards been met?

Please circle   Not at all   1   2   3   4   Totally

Comments

_____

_____

_____

_____

3. If learning has not been applied please state why

_____

_____

_____

_____

4. What further action or review is required?

_____

_____

_____

_____

Signatures _____ Participant _____ date

_____ Line manager _____ date

Index